Why doesn't somebody do something?

DAISY HEPBURN

To Betty —
Joyfully in Jesus,
Daisy Hepburn

Nehemiah 8:10

VICTOR BOOKS

a division of SP Publications, Inc.
WHEATON, ILLINOIS 60187

Offices also in Fullerton, California • Whitby, Ontario, Canada • Amersham-on-the-Hill, Bucks, England

Second printing, 1981

Scripture quotations are taken from the *New American Standard Bible* © 1960, 1962, 1963, 1968, 1971, 1972, 1973, the Lockman Foundation, La Habra, California; the King James Version; the *New International Version* © 1978 by the New York International Bible Society; *The Living Bible,* Tyndale House Publishers, Wheaton, Illinois; *The New Berkeley Version in Modern English,* © 1945, 1959, 1969 by the Zondervan Publishing House. Used by permission.

Recommended Dewey Decimal Classification: 261.6
  Suggested Subject Headings: CHURCH AND SOCIAL PROBLEMS; U.S. – MORAL CONDITIONS

Library of Congress Catalog Card Number: 80-51158
ISBN: 0-88207-606-X

VICTOR BOOKS
A division of SP Publications, Inc.
P.O. Box 1825, Wheaton, Illinois 60187

CONTENTS

Introduction

Section I   Can You Bring Good Out of Bad?
1. Leadership Calls for Sacrifice   Daisy Hepburn   **8**
2. Tax-Supported Blasphemy   Sandy Singer   **16**
3. Commitment Means
   Obedience   Fay Angus   **24**
4. A Mother Just Doesn't
   Resign   Barbara Johnson   **35**
5. Can God Use Me?   Robbi Kenney   **41**
6. Patterning for Tomorrow   Dawn Menning   **53**

Section II   Who Is Your Neighbor?
7. Disciple to the
   Disadvantaged   Kaydi Larson   **64**
8. Two Hours Each Week—
   A Civil Right   Iris Fulcher   **73**
9. Release Time Religious
   Instruction   Eleanor Sams   **78**
10. They Follow a New
    Commander   Betty Bottomly   **81**
11. Black America Is Still
    Suffering   Malettor Cross   **87**
12. Influence Is What It's
    All About   Eleanor Sams   **94**

Section III   Who Has Rights?
13. Human Life in Pieces   Julie Turnquist   **104**
14. No Guarantees on
    Freedom   Louise Matson   **110**
15. Equal Rights Amendment   **120**
16. Demanding Voices in
    a Noisy World   Gladys Dickelman   **125**

17. Prayer Is Paramount   Bev LaHaye   **135**
18. Called to Constructive
     Criticism   Norma Gabler   **142**

Section IV   Who Will Speak Up for Rights?
19. Humanism   **155**
20. Send Your Finest into
     Government   Irene Conlan   **160**
21. Christian Perspective on
     Campus   Linda Raney Wright   **166**
22. Foundation for Freedom   Martha Rountree   **174**
23. Grandma Is a Senator   Trudy Camping   **183**
24. A Flair for Priorities   Sarah Maddox   **187**

Conclusion   **199**
Suggested Reading List   **203**

Introduction

Somebody Is Doing Something!

"The wall is broken down and the gates are burned with fire!" When Nehemiah heard this, in the fifth century B.C., he decided to take action that would call for great courage, intelligence, and persistent strength. He led the people to rebuild the walls of Jerusalem, each one working near his own home.

As we enter the last two decades of the 20th century, many people in our own society are doing something near their own homes to rebuild the walls of America. They too are being asked to give great courage, intelligence, and persistent strength.

To the women whose stories are in this book, I am deeply grateful. Several of them wrote their own chapters, and the others provided me with the necessary information.

My thanks also to Victor Books editor Carole Streeter, who conceived the idea for this book and worked with me to make it a reality.

Daisy Hepburn
Felton, California
1980

Daisy Hepburn is founder/coordinator of The Hope of Our Heritage Women's Concerns and Ministries Conferences. A Bible teacher and conference speaker, Daisy is creator of the Life with Spice ministries for women, and author of nine creative Bible studies in the Life with Spice series. Daisy and her husband, David, have two children, David and Lois, and live in California. During their career, both Daisy and her husband have served as Salvation Army officers.

SECTION
I

CAN YOU BRING
GOOD OUT OF BAD?

DAISY HEPBURN and SANDY SINGER found promoters of pornographic material operating very close to their homes. FAY ANGUS took a public stand against pornography. BARBARA JOHNSON and ROBBI KENNEY had to confront the issue of homosexuality, when it affected people close to them.
DAWN MENNING faced the consuming love and stress of caring for a brain-injured child.

Nehemiah said to the people, "Don't be afraid of them. Remember the Lord, who is great and awesome, and fight for your brothers, your sons and your daughters, your wives and your homes." Nehemiah 4:14, NIV

1
Leadership Calls for Sacrifice

My arms were full of groceries on that wet October Wednesday. As I kicked open the screen, I saw a slip of paper on the door and grabbed it. After setting the sacks of groceries on the table, I did something I don't often do—I actually read the circular. It was an announcement inviting me to attend a neighborhood meeting at the new library, to discuss a city ordinance which would allow "adult" movie houses and bookstores to locate within a mile of our home.

When my husband arrived home from work a bit later, I said, "David, I think I should go to this meeting." We usually go to church on Wednesday evening.

After the dishes were washed, I halfheartedly yet dutifully went to the library. I recognized very few of the 150 people gathered there. The speaker who was "giving the facts" was a member of the City Council Planning Commission. It was evident that her view concerning the potential impact of pornography was far from mine. Following her, the state president of Morality in Media spoke.

Sitting in that meeting, I discovered something was happening to me: I was getting much more information than I wanted.

When the leader of the meeting stood, I realized he was the president of a neighborhood council—I had never attended their sessions. Shame on me! He gave the details of the action of the city council and explained what would be required to effect some change in the city ordinance to permit the "adult" houses.

When I could stand it no longer, I raised my hand and said, "I would like to offer a motion." With what I hoped was great authority, I proceeded. "I move that we draft a letter to the mayor, to the chief of police, to the city council, and anyone else who might possibly be concerned, stating that we expect the law concerning the dissemination of pornography in any form to be enforced!"

The general round of applause was punctuated by the voice of a woman who called out, "Not *expect*—but *demand!*" As she looked at me, I added quietly, "All right, *demand.*"

I knew that when the Supreme Court of the United States had handed down a definition of obscenity, the application of the law had been left to the states. In our case, the State of Minnesota would determine how to apply the definition of obscenity.

Looking directly at me, the secretary asked, "And what is your name?"

Very softly I replied, "Daisy Hepburn."

"What was that again?" he asked. "And much louder this time."

When I again replied—and this time much louder—"Daisy Hepburn," I knew in my heart of hearts that I was committed. I had just made a statement. For me it was a turning point.

I realized my commitment again, when the phone call came the next morning, asking if I approved of the wording of the letter that had been drafted in response to my motion. I don't think the neighborhood organization thought I was as committed as I felt personally, but I knew that because of my influence in a local ministry, I would would have to act on behalf of righteousness and decency. I would have to exert my influence in whatever ways God would use me, in this very important endeavor.

As I considered the need for moral renewal, I thought about building up instead of tearing down. I am not very adept at using hammers and shovels, but I have a respect for anyone who chooses to be on the construction crew rather than the demolition squad.

The Wall of Jerusalem

Thoughts about building took me back to the Bible, especially to one great builder, Nehemiah. He was a man for his time. In light of our local needs, I thought of how in his daily tasks as cupbearer to the king, Nehemiah was interrupted with the news that there was a wall to be built in Jerusalem, 1000 miles away.

The message he received was: "The wall of Jerusalem is broken down, and its gates have been burned with fire" (Neh. 1:3, NIV). When Nehemiah heard this, for some days he "mourned and fasted and prayed before the God of heaven" (1:4, NIV). Far removed from the point of need, he prayed to the Lord for an answer.

It was a prayer of praise for a faithful God who keeps His covenant of love, a prayer of confession, a prayer of remembrance of God's past faithfulness, and a prayer of petition asking God to give His servants success, as Nehemiah interceded for a needy nation. Nehemiah prayed and then dared to go in and talk to the king about the plight of the people. He told him that the walls of the city had been destroyed and left in disrepair.

When Nehemiah expressed his sadness over the condition of Jerusalem the king said, "What is it you want?"

Did I, Daisy, hear the voice of God speaking to me, as Nehemiah heard Him? "Do you, Daisy Hepburn, care enough about the condition of the protective walls in your city to become involved?"

Nehemiah had his answer. He prayed again and his response to the king was: "Send me—please send me. If it pleases the king and if your servant has found favor in his sight, send me to the city that I can rebuild it." (See Neh. 2:5.)

The idea of leaving the comfortable security of the king's own court to embark upon a 1000-mile journey that would take three months by camel, represented some sacrifice. *Leadership always demands sacrifice.* God-glorifying leadership involves a price.

Mobilizing Help

Some years ago I developed the Life with Spice programs for ladies. At this time in Minneapolis, a group of ladies, sometimes numbering 150, gathered every Thursday morning. The Life with Spice Bible study helps and creative activities provided growth opportunities. I knew that these women were as concerned about their families and neighborhoods as I was.

On that Thursday morning, I told them about my experience at the library the night before, and how I felt that the walls of protection for our homes and families were being destroyed; and that I had said, "Lord, send me to help rebuild the walls."

The ladies responded and it was decided that the next week we would pray, as Nehemiah had prayed, and then send a group of ladies to the nearest drugstore which sold pornographic magazines. One of our women was chairperson of the local elementary PTA and she had often lamented the sale of pornography from the drugstore shelves, within easy reach of children.

Six women willingly agreed to visit the manager of a nearby store the following week. With fear and trembling, and with the anticipation of doing great things for God, we embarked on our cleanup campaign.

A Beginning

The next Thursday morning, our "six mighty women" entered the drugstore. They went first to the adult magazines and selected a few. Then they approached the manager to confront him with his responsibility by showing him examples from the magazines they held.

"Well, ladies," he said, "these are so available any place that I can't get too stirred up by it. As a matter of fact, I have to put on this rack and counter what I am given. The dealers tell me that if I don't want these adult magazines, I can't get any others."

The conversation and protests continued for about 15 minutes. There was little assurance from the proprietor that any specific changes would be made. The ladies then told him that they could not shop there and would do all they could to influence other neighbors to shop elsewhere until there was a change.

After the "mighty six" returned and reported to the Life with Spice ladies, we prayed again, because we discovered in that simple act of visiting the store that we had made a beginning. We decided together that we would continue in our work.

Nehemiah also began with a visit, as he went to Jerusalem to survey the situation. After he had seen all he needed to, he said to the people, "You see the trouble we are in: Jerusalem lies in ruins, and its gates have been burned with fire. Come, let us rebuild the wall of Jerusalem, and we will no longer be in disgrace" (Neh. 2:17, NIV).

They agreed and said, "Let us begin rebuilding." So they strengthened their hands for this good work. (See Neh. 2:17-18.)

The president of Morality in Media in Minnesota is a local real estate agent who volunteers his time to MMM. He came to speak to Life with Spice about the legislative process and the pornography laws in our state. We discovered that we had been given tools with which to build. We realized too that it was the hard work of building first near our own homes that was most necessary. Our guest told us of people within our own city who were using the information available and speaking up to all concerned parties who would listen. It was good for us to hear that there were others already involved in this cleanup venture and in rebuilding.

As we continued our search for information, we found that controls on pornography often weren't applied, because the leadership of our local government did not feel that this was a crucial issue requiring high priority.

Senator Menning

We had the advantage of living close to the state capitol, and as we talked to people in government, the overwhelming reaction seemed to be, "I didn't know. I really didn't know."

State Senator Mike Menning had gone to support the building of another part of the "wall," when Anita Bryant needed help in the Dade County referendum of 1977. We asked Mike to fill us in on the pro-decency, pro-family legislation that he and several others in the state capitol had authored. We discovered that there was a growing concern in the state legislature about decency and the family.

Senator Menning invited our involvement, and even more specifically, our prayer support of a Christian coalition of state legislators, because it was going to take a miracle to turn the tide in some of the moral issues in our state.

In another quarter, a group of Christians in Minneapolis was being confronted with current issues. For 13 weeks in our adult Sunday School class, we learned about local ministries to alcoholics, to homosexuals, and to teenagers in trouble. We realized that God had allowed us to become a part of the work force, and many of us answered His "want ad." We then hoped and prayed that we could and would fulfill His job description for us.

Sandy

Sandy is a young mother of two and a homemaker by choice. In response to the challenge that one person *can* do something, Sandy asked the Lord what it was that He would have her to do. In prayer with her husband, Pete, Sandy came to the realization that since Jesus Christ lives in her, if she were to go to the state capitol and sit in on hearings for pro-decency and pro-family legislation, she would be taking the presence of God into that meeting room. With fear and trembling Sandy entered the capitol building. With her small Bible in hand, she found her way to a seat and began to learn.

Not long after that, God motivated another young woman. Soon there were three who covenanted to pray together at the capitol. Sometimes they met over coffee in the cafeteria and other times in an office of a state legislator. But most often, they quietly interceded in actual legislative committee meetings.

Sandy was one homemaker who discovered that part of the wall near her own home needed to be built. God was allowing her the privilege of putting a few bricks in the wall.

Roberta

God called Roberta to a difficult work, prayer. This requires sacrifice and dedication to the most productive work a Christian can do.

Roberta was moved by God to instigate a governmental prayer chain. This is a very disciplined group, operating by explicit rules which have been adopted for maximum effectiveness.

There are 30 women learning about legislative processes and the workings of the government. Each one prays for very specific requests and once or twice a week a 15-minute phone call going through the chain brings each of the pray-ers up to date. Once a month all 30 meet to pray together.

These ladies were seeing a dual result of their prayer work: specific answers to requests about legislation, and a profound impact on their personal lives.

Barbara

Barbara was shopping at a discount house one day, when she saw a rack of pornographic magazines that was truly rubbish!

You remember that Nehemiah and the men of Jerusalem found that having to work around the piles of rubbish consumed time and strength that they needed to get on with the building project. Of course, Barbara did not have to purchase the magazines, or even look at them. But she saw them as an alien force that was sapping the strength of people who should be building, not dragging through life. She sensed a "break in the wall" that she might have opportunity to rebuild.

As Barbara talked with the manager of the store, she found him apathetic about "just a few magazines." He had thousands of items for sale. She tried to stir the concern of other shoppers in the store, but had little success.

Going back to her church, she gathered together a few interested people and shared her concerns. Together they formed a Concerned Citizens Committee and drafted a statement which they printed on business-sized cards:

To the management: I wish you to know that I have pledged with others who share my values to end our patronage of businesses who market what we consider sexually offensive materials. We ask the support of your management to improve the moral standards of our community through your merchandising policies.

Barbara and the CCC made these cards available to people who would distribute them in bookstores and in local shopping centers. There is no way yet to measure the impact of these cards. But they represent a quiet effort to get rid of some of the rubbish that hinders the work of building.

Daisy

Now it was my turn. I visited a bookstore that was not even named "adult" and asked to see the manager. A few minutes at the magazine rack had convinced me this store was full of rubbish too.

The manager sauntered up to me and offhandedly said, "I just work here."

"Sir, I want you to know that I am offended by the magazines on this rack. I need to tell you that I plan to write the store owner, as well as the owners of this shopping plaza, because I feel that your store is misrepresenting itself. I am offended by the presence of these magazines and must do all within my influence to make sure that until something is done about them, my neighbors do not shop here."

"Lady, you are part of a minority; nobody else seems to be worried about these magazines."

Standing to my full height, I replied, "My good man, I am not part of a minority, but of a silent majority."

When I got home, I wrote three letters—one to the alderman, another to the owner of the shopping center, and the third to the owner of the bookstore. I received a reply from the alderman saying that there would be care taken to see that the pornography would not be sold in that particular shopping center. However, as of this writing, there are still 53 such magazines on that rack!

I thought again of Nehemiah, and of the many discouragements that came to his builders: their own fatigue, and malicious opposition from individuals. And yet the people kept on building.

We had made a small beginning in Minneapolis, but there was a wall to be built; and that would take time, prayer, cooperation, thought, and work. I felt almost overwhelmed by the task we had taken on.

Sandy Singer, wife, mother of two children, and homemaker, is a member of the Women's Concerns Committee of Minnesota.

2

Tax-Supported Blasphemy

The loud ring of the telephone wakened us from our early-to-bed, early-to-sleep plan. I responded sleepily to the insistent voice coming through the wire, "Daisy, we have received a highly offensive issue of the *University of Minnesota Daily*. It was planned to be an end-of-year humor edition. Instead, it is a blasphemous, pornographic assault on the cross and the church. We are asking people to meet on the Northrup Mall about 7 o'clock tomorrow night for a protest demonstration. The media have been invited, and we are hoping for a good turnout of concerned citizens. If you have time to make a large sign before you come, please bring it along!"

I turned over to my husband, and relayed the message. Sleep eluded me for a few minutes while I pondered what might be in a university-sponsored newspaper that would elicit that kind of action. *Oh well, tomorrow is another day.*

Protest Demonstration

We had neither time nor inclination to make a sign. But we did arrive the next evening, just after a simple march of protest had taken place. We were not disappointed to have missed it—we just don't seem to be the sign-carrying, protest-marching type. Even when I heard that the

Have You Been Nailed?

Metal workers trade publication seeks interviews with persons recently crucified for piercing article on galvanized nail side effects. Short Jewish males preferred.

Nails and Screws Journal
Mines and Metallurgy
202 Morrill Hall

admi... ...lected ...and demand the ... Where's the can
yea. The currently si ...write to y... Christ's somebody says this to
led up career ...crap out of 'em and
0 sacks. later.

Sex and the Busy student

Hey, once and for all, are Jim *religion.*
abors and Rock Hudson fags or

Attention: Lust-inclined

When a cold shower doesn't do the trick, cr
Ice-cold Bethlehem steel
Listen to testimoni

• "The lamb's skin liner cuts do"

• "Beats hell out of imm"

• "I'd be burned

Holy Christ!

He sure is. And now you can get the Savior and all your favorite Christian Stars with Matthew's Bubble Gum Holy Cards.

Jesus wows 'em on the Mall as he cracks a funny one.

pornographic film *Deep Throat* had been sponsored at the university, and learned that other similar films were part of their film library, I tried to forget about it, feeling that one person could not really alter the course of the entire University of Minnesota.

A small group, surely not more than 40 people, was gathered on the lawn. A microphone had been set up and the group listened as a recent graduate of the university spoke with concern about the newspaper and how ashamed she was of it. The media were not paying much attention. A member of the ad hoc committee which had formed to protest the edition thrust fliers in our hands. The flier consisted of quotes and excerpts from this issue of the *Minnesota Daily*. We were stunned! As we read our faces flushed with anger mixed with embarrassment. I believe it is safe to say that we, as middle-aged adults, had never before been confronted with such blatant blasphemy.

"Will someone here please tell me what everyone is so upset about?" a curly-headed young man student asked. We recognized him as the one who had interviewed the costumed student, dressed to represent Jesus, on the campus mall. The picture of the interview, with the cross leaned against a card table, was on the center page of the *Daily*. The conversation with "Christ" in the "Today's Stupid" column had taken place in the shadow of the university's Northrup Auditorium.

"What is the big problem?" he inquired.

My husband answered first. "Young man, it is evident that you do not know who Jesus Christ is. Let me say that if this humor had been aimed at any number of leading citizens or heroes of your generation, black or white, there would have been a demonstration on this campus that would never have been forgotten."

My friend Sandy Singer spoke with emotion: "There has never been such an expression of love as that shown on Calvary, when God commended His love toward us, and Christ died for us while we were yet sinners. My Saviour was never flybait-on-a-stick!"

"Dear young man," I added, "have you ever met Jesus Christ? Have your mother and father ever taken you to church or Sunday School? Do you know the One about whom you are speaking in these articles?"

The conversation went on for a few minutes more, but we knew that we had not seen or heard the end of this irreverent attack by the student newspaper.

State Senate Committee

Several days later, a special committee challenged the governor of the state of Minnesota, Albert Quie, to take some action in regard to the tax support of the University of Minnesota, specifically as it related to its student publication. When we heard that this special committee of the Minnesota Senate was going to meet, my husband and I went to the state capitol. The chairman of the Board of Regents and the university president testified.

It was unnerving to observe the TV cameras picking up these testimonies, and then just a few hours later to watch the evening news and see selected phrases and paragraphs from their testimonies, which were evidently slanted toward the opinion of the news media. It seemed to the television viewer that the president was apologizing—perhaps condoning—or at least sympathizing with the students who he felt ought not to be judged too harshly. However, in his testimony before the senate, he had indicated that he was appalled and embarrassed by the issue of the *Daily*. But his closing remarks presented on TV were, "May we be careful not to be out of balance when it comes to the consideration and final judgment or disposition of this case, and as it relates to the First Amendment provision."

As we were leaving the capitol building that afternoon, we had a few moments with several Christian state senators, as well as the state president of Morality in Media. They affirmed something which we have learned to be the case: "The First Amendment of our Constitution does not provide for blasphemy or obscenity."

Sandy's Clarion Voice

Sandy Singer who was at the Northrup Mall during the simple demonstration, and present at the capitol for the hearing, related her experience:

"It was to be an informative hearing. Before I knew it, I was on the schedule to testify. Testifying before a senate committee was one thing I thought I would never do; but, as a Christian, I couldn't keep silent. On the day of the hearing, the committee room was packed—wall to wall with people. Many Christians had come, and they were just there to pray. Many university students were there also.

"When my turn came to testify, I shared from my heart what Jesus means to me. I explained how, as Christians, we felt it was totally unjust to expect us to pay for the mocking of our Saviour. I trembled that day as I have never trembled before; but there were Christians all around me who were praying—praying that Jesus would give me the words, praying that He would unplug the ears of the senators and soften their hearts. What a wonderful comfort! That day was a day of confirmation for me also. I had been asked by a pro-life organization to be a lobbyist for them; but, after testifying, I knew that the Lord had me where He wanted to use me—that is, in a prayer ministry.

"Speaking with one of the senators a few weeks ago, I found out that prayer is still a priority with them. Even as I write this tonight, they are on the Christian coalition legislators' annual retreat. In the midst of prayer and Bible study, they draft legislation. This year they will be looking at the *Minnesota Daily* issue to see what legislation they can draft to cut off the public funding. It's going to mean changing the constitution of the state to accomplish this, but we know that in Jesus' power it can be done. For sure, we will be in each committee hearing, praying, and if the Lord directs, testifying. Just in case, I have recently taken a persuasive public speaking class."

Identification Is Commitment

Sandy had found out that identification is commitment—much like I found that day in the library when I was asked to give my name louder and realized that identifying myself at that moment was a commitment. I had made a statement about where I stood, and now I was expected to act on that statement. I don't know that anybody else had those expectations of me, but I have found that when I articulate a deep decision or commitment, I sense a strong motivation to make sure that my words are acted out in my life.

Perhaps that is why I identify myself with Simon Peter, who tended to put his foot in his mouth. The idea of carrying a sign and marching in a protest demonstration is not very appealing to me, but I am confident that God is able to motivate us as Christians to make good on our commitments in the most effective manner.

I am reminded of the words of Eugenia Price. When asked to write an article about her commitment to Christ, she said, "No, I have said too much already about my commitment to God. I have decided to write about God's commitment to me." May we not forget that God has committed to us all that we need—and more—to act obediently.

Sandy's Senate Testimony

Mr. Chairman, my name is Mrs. Peter Singer. I am a housewife and mother of two children. I am also a member of the Temple

Baptist Church in St. Paul and a member of the Women's Concerns Committee of Minnesota. This committee represents hundreds of women throughout our state. Also, I speak to you on behalf of myself; I am a Christian and a taxpayer.

I feel that my Christian belief has been mocked, ridiculed, and defamed. The taxes that I have paid in this state have been intentionally abused by the *Minnesota Daily*. I am urging you today to institute legislation that will halt any future state subsidy of the *Minnesota Daily*.

The *Minnesota Daily* has spoken at length today about First Amendment Rights. I certainly would be the last one to support the removal of anyone's rights. But I would like to ask you, "What about my rights?" I have been forced as a taxpaying citizen to finance a paper which has intentionally attacked my Lord and Saviour, Jesus Christ. I know of no other member of the media that has gone to such lengths to maliciously attack the Christian faith.

My tax dollars, either directly or indirectly (whichever does not really matter, since the money gets there either way) have helped to finance this vicious attack.

When I speak to you about the malicious attack that has been made upon my faith, I feel that it is important for you to realize what Christians mean when they speak about their faith. If you understand that, maybe you will understand why we are responding to this issue of the *Daily*.

We do not speak of faith in God in the same way that we speak of faith in George Washington. I do believe in George Washington, and I believe that he was a real person, but I am not expecting George Washington to do anything for me right now. My faith in Jesus is much different—much more. It is placing my trust in Jesus and what He did for me 2,000 years ago on the cross. We have placed all our weight upon Jesus as Christians, and we are relying on Him alone to hold us up as righteous before God. Jesus is our whole life.

Now you see what has been done here by the *Minnesota Daily*. They have taken the Old Rugged Cross, and they have made a dirty joke out of it. When they got done with their dirty joke, they expected us to laugh at it. We love the cross. It was on that cross that our dear Saviour died. Is it not enough that we helped to finance this attack? Must we also be expected to laugh at it?

School is a place where we transmit our culture. Does the *Minnesota Daily* properly reflect our culture? In the name of humor and satire in our culture, is it permissible to portray God as a whore? In the name of humor and satire in our culture, is it permissible to portray the mother of Jesus as one who endorses masturbation devices? In the name of humor and satire, it is permissible to call the greatest act of love that the world has ever known "flybait-on-a-stick"?

I hope that the *Minnesota Daily* is not an accurate reflection of the culture that is being transmitted at the university. Because the *Minnesota Daily* is looked upon as a leader—and we have heard testimony today that it is quoted in university publications across our country—then is there not all the more reason for it to be top quality, not smut? Is this paper worthy of our tax dollars?

I urge you to demonstrate respect for my rights as a taxpayer, by introducing legislation which will not in any way support the *Minnesota Daily*. In this way, you will restore my rights as a tax-paying citizen.

—To a State of Minnesota special senate committee
July 1979, St. Paul, Minnesota

No Time for Detours

In Nehemiah's account of building, we read of his enemies' scheme to harm him. He had the wisdom to decline their invitation to meet them on the plains. "I am carrying on a great project and cannot go down" (Neh. 6:3, NIV). One of the things that hampers our effectiveness and gives delight to the enemy of our souls is our lack of respect for the job that God has called us to do.

There is a great work to be done. What does it matter if the place to be filled is a small one? When the enemy invites you to meet him, respond, "This is a great project I am working on and I will not be sidetracked, even to defend myself."

Jesus Christ was free of the need to defend Himself. His mission was high and holy and He did not get sidetracked by the need to defend that mission.

My husband picked up a phrase that he uses to encourage me at crucial moments in my life—those moments when I am tempted to throw in the towel and give in to the enticing temptation of discouragement or conciliation with the enemy. I don't think it is original, but it packs a wallop every time. "Daisy," he will say, "you need a higher hill than that to die on." When I begin a great project, I must not be drawn downward into lesser things. God has called us to a great work and it is a "high hill." We find it so easy to settle for second best. But God wants us to devote our energy to a work worthy of our life's investment, even unto death—a hill high enough—a hill worth taking!

When the job in Jerusalem was done, when the wall was built, the people had a reason to celebrate. When we see small victories, we too have reason to celebrate. It is essential that we not consider our work to be of little value, for it is what God asks us to do. As we are faithfully His people in the world, we will have our reward. And we will see the results of change in the lives of individuals and in society.

One person *can* make a difference. One woman who cares *can* bring some good from a bad situation. Sandy did in Minnesota, and you can in your neighborhood, because you are somebody special.

Fay Angus was born in Australia, has spent time in China and Japan, and now lives in California. Wife, mother, and concerned citizen, Fay is a conference speaker and pro-decency leader, and has authored several books, including The White Pagoda *and* The Catalyst.

3
Commitment Means Obedience

Fay Angus is a woman to be reckoned with—but her wit and charm are so disarming that even the formidable foes she has debated on pornography and the homosexual movement have been caught off guard!

Fay is the mother of a boy and a girl, and wife of a Canadian engineer. She was born in Australia, raised in Shanghai, China, and spent more than two years in a Japanese concentration camp.

The White Pagoda is the story of her life in China, her imprisonment, and her subsequent move to Canada. But it is in this excerpt from her book *Up to Heaven, Down to Earth,* the sequel to *Between Your Status and Your Quo!* that I most identify with Fay:

This summer I decided to concentrate on complete victory in memorizing Scripture. "Satan does not want us memorizing God's Word," I told the family. "He fogs our minds and muddles our memory. Well, are we going to let the devil get the better of us?"

The kids were rolling their eyes . . . totally unappreciative of original oratory!

"Not only will we win the victory, but I will offer $2 a dozen for memorized proverbs!"

I thought of all the juicy ones I'd zap into their psyche!

Within a week Ian shrugged up to me. The "shrug" is the latest 11-year-old strut—he jiggled his shoulders and shuffled his feet. "How much will you pay for three proverbs?"

"Nothing," I snapped back, "nothing flat. It's a dozen or zero, Z-E-R-O!"

A wicked gleam came into his eyes. "Well, if you won't pay me for the three proverbs, how much will you pay me to forget I ever read Song of Solomon?"

I whacked him hard (Regal, p. 31).

Fay's Story

I had every reason to be afraid. Carmine Galante had just been gunned down in New York. Joe Colombo had been shot the previous year. They were both on the chart. So were Joe Bonnano, Mike Zaffarano, Reuben Sturman, and other big guns of organized crime. Thevis, Hamling, Luros, Greenlin, Goldstein, Paladina—79 key names and locations in a web spun across the United States, connecting people involved in the $4-billion-a-year business of hard-core pornography.

Homer Young of the FBI had given me permission to use the chart. His years with the Bureau as coordinator of their field division handling obscenity investigation nationwide had made him one of the men most respected and feared by the Mafia. He is retired now but has not given up the fight. He continues to share his knowledge and speak out on the issues. His son wears Homer's badge now and carries on his dad's work with the FBI in California.

I was scheduled to hold up the chart and expose organized crime's control of the porno trade in an interview with former L.A. Mayor Sam Yorty on his TV show in just a few weeks. Several million American viewers would see the show and hear the truth. Hard-core porno is CRIME, organized crime. Hard-core porno is the MAFIA involvement. It is not the buxom girlie magazine, nor the odd X-rated movie. Hard-core porno is depravity and one of the vilest degeneracies ever exhibited by the human race!

Am I in Danger?

"Yeah, sure Mom," said my young son Ian. "We're gonna come home someday and find you swinging on the old oak tree in the driveway with both your legs broken!"

I phoned the police chief in Pasadena. His vice and narcotics squad had come to one of our community task force meetings to "educate" us on just what was available in the several hard-core houses on Colorado Boulevard in the beautiful City of Roses. I had come to know him well and admired him tremendously.

"No," he said. "They'd be stupid to do anything to you."

I agreed; they'd be stupid to kill a martyr for the cause.

I phoned Homer. "Am I in any danger, Homer?" I asked. "Would they come after me?"

"Fay, you're nothing to them but a feather floating in the breeze!" Homer went on to explain that the Mafia had everything so completely controlled and tied up that one little lady was nothing but a laughable threat.

A feather floating in the breeze, eh? I thought. *Well, what they may not realize is that one feather, plus one feather, plus one feather makes an American eagle. And the American eagle is the emblem of freedom for the American people. The people are the voice, and as the people speak, and as the people legislate, and as the people vote, so moves the country! I'd better start collecting feathers.*

I fell to my knees. "O God," I prayed, "I'm not afraid of failing; I'm only afraid of never trying. Help me to wake up people, Your people. And through the power of Your Holy Spirit and the authority of Your Word, cleanse our land!"

I did the Yorty interview. We got a phone call late the night it was aired. A vile, blasphemous phone call.

Some weeks earlier I had spoken at an anti-porno rally at the Hollywood Knickerbocker Hotel—right on the Strip, a couple of blocks from the infamous Plato's Retreat West. *Screw West* magazine had their reporters at the rally and did a distorted, splashy write-up in their next issue. They said we had "mental arthritis." It was somewhat unnerving to find one's name on the same page as a picture of a naked bride with a bouquet of flowers in her groin.

I was to run into Goldstein of *Screw West* again later, much later! His is one of the most depraved porno rags sold in vending machines on the city streets of the West Coast where for 50¢ any child can purchase it and fill his mind with smut.

Commitment

Now that I had taken a public stand against pornography through the media, there was no turning back.

I have always believed that if you stick your neck out you'll see more of the world. Unfortunately, you also run the risk of getting your head chopped off! That's the good news/bad news of active social involvement. I was seeing a whole lot of a world I'd rather not see. And my neck was getting stretched.

"Firm up my commitment, Lord," I prayed. The summary of Christian commitment comes in one word—OBEDIENCE!

Obedience! The response that moves us out from the personalized walk of faith so often cloaked in the convenience of our familiar and comfortable lifestyles.

Obedience! Frequently moving us up and out into unfamiliar, inconvenient, and disturbing ways of life. I often found myself in the sheer panic of peculiar circumstances through which the Holy Spirit of God performs His purposes through my availability.

Obedience means being pulled into the nitty gritty by the clear command, "But be ye doers of the Word, and not hearers only" (James 1:22a, KJV). Obedience means being motivated away from apathy and into action.

The greatest ally of degeneracy is apathy. That fact prompted Edmund Burke to write, "All that is necessary for the forces of evil to win in the world is for enough good men (and women) to do nothing."

My own commitment to obey, and the surrender of my personal preferences to the whatever, whenever, wherever, and however of God's will, have taken me down many paths I would rather not have walked. Now they were causing me to look at things I'd rather never see.

"How on earth did a gentle lady like you ever get into the fight against pornography?" That question follows me through every interview.

Obedience is the only answer—obedience in response to the facts, information, and confirming circumstances brought into my life by the leading of the Holy Spirit.

Church Women United

My involvement against pornography started with a Church Woman United forum in Pasadena. Ray Gauer of Citizens for Decency through Law was the speaker.

"Something *can* be done," said Ray. "The people of this nation *do not* have to accept the violation of their community standards by pornographic theatres, bookstores, and vending machines on their city streets." He went on to explain that the Supreme Court had never upheld that obscenity was covered by First Amendment rights.

"One solution to the problem is through community involvement," Ray continued. He's a man who knows his stuff. Ray Gauer has devoted over 20 years of his life to raising a standard for decency in America. A powerful speaker, his stocky figure radiates conviction, and he puts the power of his faith behind it. In his position as assistant to Congressman Robert Dornan for many years, he added to his experience the expertise of knowing the legislative processes. Thank God for men like Gauer and Charles Keating, the founder of Citizens for Decency through Law.

The forum is a source of information exchange. Some information may be mentally filed as an additive to the education of the whole person; other information prods for action. Church Women United decided to act and I found myself a part of that action.

Following Ray's suggestion for community involvement, we sent to all our local legislators, to our police chiefs of surrounding cities, and to churches and organizations such as the PTA, Scouts, Rotary, etc., the following invitation:

> With the help of Citizens for Decency through Law, Church Women United in the greater Pasadena area are pulling together a community task force with a view to eliminating the blight of pornography from our city streets.
>
> With confidence in the moral standards of your organization, we invite your concerned representation on this task force.
>
> At a recent meeting with Pasadena Police Chief Robert McGowan, we pledged our support in his open and publicized crackdown on crime, prostitution, and pornography.
>
> The city of San Pedro has joined many other cities throughout the nation in successfully eliminating all adult theatres and porno bookstores from their communities—why can't we? We believe we can, and we solicit your help!
>
> (We gave details of date, time, place of meeting, etc.)
>
> We enclose a list of organizations to whom this letter is being addressed and will appreciate your indication of participation by your prompt return of the RSVP form.

The response was excellent and a task force was organized. We had grabbed the tiger by the tail. Now we started to pull. Gauer, with the help of Jim Clancy, one of the nation's top antiobscenity lawyers, developed a "Community Standards" initiative to activate the legislative process. It is an initiative that continues to be successfully passed in many states across the nation.

NOTE: *Initiative* is "a procedure enabling a specified number of voters by petition to propose a law and secure its submission to the electorate or to the legislature for approval" *(Webster's New Collegiate Dictionary).* An initiative so generated, or a measure passed or proposed by a legislative body, may then be submitted to popular vote in a *referendum.*

We had only three weeks in which to obtain 350,000 signatures to get the initiative on the ballot for the upcoming election that year. Unfortunately, we didn't make it in time, and are going through the process again. But action had started.

Need for Cleansing

Looking at hard-core pornography was the really tough assignment for me.

"How do you cope?" people asked. "Pornography is so vile!"

They were right, it was vile and at first I didn't cope at all. I saw the bondage pictures of women trussed up like animals with baseballs gagging their mouths, or strung up to be whipped, or turned upside down ready to be sodomized with a whip handle. One was even bound to a cross. The models looked so young. I started praying for the models. Looking at the children was the worst of all.

I wept a lot and had a few weeks of nightmares. Then came the cleansing.

"God, give me a clinical mind," I prayed. I thought of my dear friend Doctor Merton, on emergency room duty for so many years. In the trauma of the medical profession, he dealt so frequently with human depravity and its consequences.

Philippians 4:8 became my lifeline to sanity. "Finally, brethren, whatsoever things are true, whatsoever things are honest, whatsoever things are just, whatsoever things are pure, whatsoever things are lovely, whatsoever things are of good report; if there be any virtue, and if there be any praise, think on these things" (KJV).

Lovely things, things of "good report"—these were to fill my mind. God took His Word and used it as a windshield wiper to cleanse my mind, time after time. And, praise Him, He did indeed give me the clinical attitude I so desperately needed for this work.

Commitment Means Obedience

I had the free will to say, "No, Lord." I did, many times. Eventually, my wincing hesitation and shaky "I'll try" were strengthened by His Holy Spirit to a point of totally uncompromising and confident trust in a God who lived in me through the promise of Christ: "We will come unto him and make Our abode with him" (John 14:23c, KJV). Confident trust in a God whose plan for His will in and through my life, was far beyond my own limited vision.

"Translate my weaknesses into Your strength," became my daily prayer. I appropriated into my life God's words to Joshua: "Have not I commanded thee? Be strong and of a good courage; be not afraid, neither be thou dismayed; for the Lord thy God is with thee whithersoever thou goest" (Josh. 1:9 KJV).

This was a commandment, not an option. *Be* strong, *be* not dismayed or afraid. "I am with you," said my Lord.

Obedience! This call to action in my life became the challenge to raise up a standard for biblical morality that was to enlarge over the weeks and months ahead.

I thank God we never have to apologize for our biblical morality. God the Father knew exactly what He was doing when He made the rules, and they have total sociological credibility.

Promiscuity has led us into VD pandemic (totally out of control) across the nation, with gonorrhea of the mouth and throat now epidemic. New strains of VD are developing that do not respond to the antibiotics available.

Perversions of sodomy, incest, pedophilia (sexual orientation with the child as the preferred object), and bestiality are raising their self-interest groups in a concerted effort to corrupt the sexuality of America.

A few years ago humorist Erma Bombeck parodied: "God give me the courage to change what can be changed, God give me the patience to endure what cannot be changed, and God give me the wisdom to *keep my mouth shut when I don't know the difference!*"

I thank God that as Christians we do know the difference. But far too many of us have kept our mouths shut for too long!

A Generation for Decisions

I believe we are living in one of the most exciting and challenging periods in the entire history of civilization. I believe that this generation is facing moral decisions that could well change the course

of human destiny—decisions about life-manipulative issues.
- Gerontic extension of life—the possibility of science controlling growth and aging hormones to extend our individual spans 200-300 years.
- Genetic engineering—the test-tube baby with a positive result that couples previously unable to have children may now conceive; and a negative result that lesbians are demanding reproductive freedom to bear children through artificial insemination.
- Baby recipes—predetermining the sex of a child through out-of-the-womb fertilization. If you don't get what you want, slosh! Down the drain it goes!
- Abortion—denying the right of a fetus to be considered a person who is afforded human dignity from the point of conception.
- The age of sexual consent—controlled legislatively at the traditional acceptance of 18 years, and now being lowered in some states to 14 (Iowa). New Jersey tried for 13 (this was rescinded by the people's outrage). Germany has made it 15. And there are advocates suggesting ages 4 to 16!
- The homosexual's right to marry.
- Incest—with the acceptance of intra-family sex and the suggestion that there is nothing wrong with a man using his whole family sexually.
- Prostitution—an advocacy for its decriminalization, slogans coming out of Australia saying, "Marriage is only a poorly paid form of prostitution," the COYOTE group of prostitutes in San Francisco promoting a name that stands for *C*ast *O*ff *Y*our *O*ld *T*raditional *E*thics.
- Decisions on the rights of children to divorce their parents, decisions on what constitutes perversion, decisions about bestiality, obscenity, and pornography.
- Decisions that will be made in legislative bodies of countries around the world and that will be contested by various self-interest groups and fought over through the judiciary systems of the courts.

Moral Decisions
A reporter once asked me, "Mrs. Angus, what do you mean by *moral?* Morality is relative. Will you define morality for us?"

"Certainly," I replied. *"Moral* is a word that comes from the Latin root *mores* meaning "habits," the habits of a culture, the habits of a society, the habits of a nation. Morality is the acceptable, habitual behavior of a culture; immorality *(immores)* is the unacceptable, habitual behavior of a culture."

"Ah-h, but can you legislate morality?" he continued.

This is one of the questions that I am most frequently asked on the public platform, and yet this is the question that has the most factual answer.

The criminal laws legislated in penal codes around the world are *legislated moral laws*—laws on behavior habits which are acceptable or unacceptable within a culture.

Polygamy, acceptable in some cultures, is legislated as an unacceptable habit, or immoral, in the United States of America. Bigamy, prostitution, incest, sodomy, and bestiality are all legislated as immoral in most states of the Union. I would like to see pornography legislated as immoral and unacceptable as well!

The responsibility of these moral decisions is carried by the voting public, and is transmitted through our elected representatives. I believe one of the greatest mission fields in the world today is the legislative body of a nation. We need a clarion call to the Christian community to get involved.

We stand before the firing squad of those self-interest groups who seek to break down traditional moral values. Their belabored anthem is the First Amendment—freedom of speech and freedom of the press.

But I quote from Chief Justice of the United States Warren Burger, when he ruled against a pornographer in 1973 (California vs. Miller): "To equate the free and robust exchange of ideas and political debate with commercial exploitation of obscene material demeans the grand conception of the First Amendment and its high purposes in the historic struggle for freedom. It is a misuse of the great guarantees of free speech and free press."

We all need to march in the equal rights movements that bring worth, honor, and dignity to every member of the human race, regardless of ethnic origin. However, we are now being bombarded by the *equal wrongs* movements, with the erotic drumbeat of the prostitute cause, the homosexual/lesbian platforms, and the overbalance of child advocacy that demands rights for children to divorce their parents or not to attend church even in early formative years. We hear of equal wrongs from the pedophiliac who says there is nothing abnormal in his sexual preference for children—he says it is society that has erroneously dubbed it wrong. And from the Guyon

Society with its slogan: "Sex by Eight or It's Too Late!" Are these equal rights or *equal wrongs?*

All our *rights* are governed rights. All our *freedoms* are governed freedoms. That is what makes government so important. Try driving a car totally free of laws and see how far you get. Try standing up in Congress and yelling four-letter words at the president, in exercise of your freedom of speech, and see how long you last! Functional freedom is disciplined and controlled. God the Father knew that when He made the rules.

In the United States we now have an estimated 300,000 to 600,000 teenage prostitutes. One little girl of eight in California, trained by *her father* to be a prostitute, earned $1,000 a night.

Dr. Judianne Dennson Gerber, one of the national authorities on the sexual abuse of children, has testified concerning cases of gonorrhea of the throat in children two years old and younger. She stated in a broadcast over the Physicians Radio Network (New York) that physicians observing unusual throat complaints in small children should check for gonorrhea.

We have an annual count of over one million teenage pregnancies nationally—6,000 in girls 12 years old and under. More than 30,000 children in the greater Los Angeles area alone have been used in child pornography; this count explodes to near one-half million nationwide.

Optimism and Action

I am so frequently asked, "Fay, don't you ever get discouraged or feel pessimistic about the state of our world?"

My answer is "No, never!"

Golda Meir was asked during a TV interview, "Golda, don't you ever feel pessimistic about the state of Israel?"

Golda turned her dark eyes towards the camera and said, "The people of Israel cannot afford to take the time to feel pessimistic about anything. The people of Israel have too much to do!"

As Christians placed here at this specific time of history, for God's specific purposes, we too cannot afford to take the time to feel pessimistic about anything, for we also have too much to do! Let's get into the action.

We need to ask ourselves, "If not I—who? If not now—when? If not here—where?"

If you and I do not take a stand for biblical morality, tell me, who will? And facing the facts, we must agree that we are already somewhat late. If we don't do it now, tell me, when should we start? And as believers, carrying the standard of Jesus Christ wherever we go, if we don't do it in the communities where we live, tell me, where should we begin?

Ariel Durant, who together with her husband Wil Durant wrote the 11-volume *Story of Civilization,* was once asked if in all her research and experience there was a woman who stood out uniquely as having contributed the most to civilization.

Without a moment's hesitation she answered, "Not a woman, but women! The women of the 13th century." She went on to explain how at that brutal time of history those women preserved education and culture, preserved their religious convictions and morality, and literally turned around the course of a degenerate society.

When the history of this generation is written, I pray that it will be recorded that Christian men and the women around the world preserved the family, and preserved education and culture through religious convictions and biblical morality that turned the course of human destiny.

My father left me a quotation from Sir Francis Drake. It was written in 1587 and continues to be true even today.

Men pass away, but people abide. See that ye hold fast the heritage we leave you. Yea, and teach your children its value, that never in the coming centuries their hearts may fail them or their hands grow weak. Hitherto, we have been too much afraid. Henceforth we will fear only God.

Oh Lord God, when Thou givest to Thy servants to endeavor any great matter, grant us to know that it is not the beginning but the continuing of the same until it be thoroughly finished which yieldeth the true glory; through Him who for the finishing of Thy work laid down His life, our Redeemer, Jesus Christ. Amen.

Barbara Johnson, wife and mother, is the founder of Spatula Ministries of La Habra, California and author of Where Does a Mother Go to Resign?

4
A Mother Just Doesn't Resign

En route to a holiday retreat weekend, Barbara Johnson with two of her four sons, drove up through the hills of Southern California, her car loaded down with groceries and bedding. It was dark and roads were reported to be washed out along the route, due to a heavy rainstorm. The headlights revealed a mound in the middle of the road that turned out to be a man's form. Barb stopped the car and investigated. To her horror she saw that it was her own husband lying there, his body torn and bleeding. In the hours that followed, Barbara experienced a supernatural self-control that enabled her to find help, guide the ambulance to the hospital, and watch as they wheeled Bill into the emergency room.

Her heart sank, however, when the doctors gave her the prognosis. Bill had sustained so much brain damage that he would be totally disabled.

God was preparing Barbara for even greater trials, using this time in her life to show His strength perfected in Barbara's weakness. God gave her patience, persistence, courage, and especially, success. The tender healing power of God flowed to Bill from Barbara and the boys in encouraging ways. Bill slowly regained strength and two years later he returned to his work as a mechanical engineer.

God knew that Bill was going to be needed in the days still ahead, when the family experienced blow after blow beating down upon them.

Family Grieving

Barbara's second son Steve was only 18 when he joined the Marines in 1968. It was just a few months later when Barbara felt compelled to get up early one July morning to write Steve a letter of spiritual encouragement and affirmation. She sent it to Vietnam where he was involved in a terrorizing battle. He was so young, and the vision of the glory of war faded quickly when he arrived in the thick of the fight.

Steve was killed on July 28. Barbara received word that Steve had gotten her letter the day before his death. He had lain face down in a rice paddy for two days before his body was picked up. Ten days later his casket was brought home. Bill was not able to face the trauma of identifying his son, so Barbara went alone to the mortuary.

"Safe in the Arms of Jesus" had been sung during the farewell service for the servicemen as they left earlier that year, and Barbara rested in the fact that Steve had been secure in his knowledge of Christ as Saviour and was now right there in the presence of Jesus!

Tim, the oldest, was an adventurer. In 1973, he set out with two friends, Ron and Al, for a summer of exploring Alaska. They had big hopes of making some fast money and were elated at the prospects before them.

When their little car was being serviced in a gas station in Anchorage, a mechanic named Ted talked to the three young men about Jesus. None of them were living for Christ at the time, but providentially, they all went home with Ted for dinner and stayed five weeks! While living and learning with Ted, the young men's lives took root in the love of Jesus, and they grew spiritually by leaps and bounds.

Tim wrote home and told his mother what had happened to him. "This trip has been fantastic! I've had a chance to do a lot of deep thinking; burdens have been lifted. I have peace of mind—it's wonderful!"

Barbara and Bill were awed at the change in their son, and excitedly awaited his return. "I'm on my way home," Tim called to tell them, as they left the Yukon territory. A head-on collision took Tim and Ron right into the presence of the Lord Jesus, within a few hours after that phone call.

Once again Barbara went to the mortuary to identify a son's body. Once again, God confirmed to her heart that He had everything under control. There were low moments however!

"As I stood in that mortuary, waiting to identify Tim's broken body, I was reliving an old, bad dream. This was the very same room, the same wallpaper, the same carpeting, the same everything—except here was another box with another boy in it. So unreal! How unbelievable that this could happen to me twice!"

Shock Waves

In June of 1975, as the family was anticipating a visit from relatives and a trip to Disneyland, they were hit by another devastating blow.

Barbara had recovered, in her words, "better than could have been expected" from the numerous tragedies that had struck her family. Her own pastor had been able to refer parents to her for help with grief in their own lives.

But this was too much! On that summer afternoon, Barb had occasion to go to son Larry's room where she found magazines and letters, books, and other shocking materials to indicate that Larry was far too interested in homosexuality.

"My head felt like a pressure cooker about to explode. How could I let him know that I had found the magazines, and still go through with our plans for Disneyland that evening? I wrote him a hurried note: 'Larry, I saw the magazines and stuff in your room. I love you and God loves you, but this is so wrong. Can we just get through tonight and, after the relatives leave tomorrow, talk about it? Please meet us at the flagpole at Disneyland at 8 o'clock so we can enjoy the parade and fireworks with them anyway.'"

Larry met the family in the midst of the crowd at Disneyland, and in those surroundings full of cheering and celebration, he blurted out, with eyes full of tears, "I'm a homosexual—maybe a bisexual."

Gathering strength and courage, she simply hugged him and reaffirmed the love she and Bill had for him. But inside, Barbara was churning, in search of some way to disappear from the face of the earth. But where *does* a mother go to resign?

Survival

Barbara began a pilgrimage through mountains and valleys, depression and disappointment, screams and survival, love and hate. Information was what she needed—but how was she to get it?

Were there no other mothers who had shared the same trauma—Christians or not? With the rising tide of gay people "coming out of the closet," Barbara knew that there had to be others with whom she could share this heaviest of all burdens.

Larry had confessed Christ as a child, and was quick to declare his love for the Lord. How this could happen was a terrible mystery to her. Barbara, in desperation, began to visit a Christian psychologist. He encouraged her to keep a log of her experience, and she wrote and wrote and wrote "survival notes." In some of her better moments, she could imagine God using even this experience to help others—but where *were* the others?

Love in Action, a ministry to homosexuals in San Rafael, California, was brought to her attention. Frank Worthen, from this most successful ministry, was immeasurably helpful to her. He not only gave her much-needed information, but large doses of encouragement as well.

In a quiet but helpful way, son number four Barney and husband Bill became a support system for Barbara. Their friends at Melodyland Church in Anaheim undergirded the family as well.

Barbara remembered the many occasions, after the deaths of her other sons, when Christian friends had brought food, had given assurances of prayers, and had demonstrated their love and concern in countless ways. This was different. Larry was alive, and there were no friends calling at the door, no hot dishes being brought to their kitchen. But through the long months, Barbara again had the opportunity to see God fulfilling His promises to her—promises to comfort, sustain, protect, and even after a long separation, to bring Larry back into communication with his parents.

Start of a Ministry

Stemming from personal experience, Barbara founded Spatula Ministries. This ministry to parents got its name one evening as Barbara sat in a meeting at the Hotline Counseling Center (a ministry of Melodyland). Each person in the group was asked what he needed to make his ministry more effective. Barb, with characteristic wit, said, "Well, I need about a dozen big spatulas to pull these frantic mothers down off the ceiling when they first learn their kids are homosexuals!" Spatula Ministries provides printed information and cassette tapes, as well as opportunities to interact with others facing this family crisis.

One helpful piece of literature provided by Spatula Ministries is entitled "When Homosexuality Hits Your Home":

1. Stop blaming yourself! You cannot take blame for the choice your child has made. Remove self-pity by realizing that there is no one factor identified as the root cause of homosexuality.

2. Don't try to give advice. Rather than play the counselor/psychologist role, unconditionally love and accept your child through his/her struggles with identity.

3. Start a "Joy Box" collection of inspirational verses and poems to help lighten those days you feel the fog of depression settling in.

4. Keep communication channels open with your child—even if he's left home. If you've blown your initial confrontation, reach out to him in love, admitting you made a mistake in overreacting.

5. Concentrate on making your home a warm, loving place for the rest of your family.

6. Get involved in a praise-centered church, in a prayer cell, in hobbies, tape ministries, and with helping other people through their suffering. This brings your focus outside of yourself and your suffering.

7. Praise the Lord continually in the *midst of* the situation. Believe He knows the end result—and will bring good out of it.

8. Find a friend with whom you can share, laugh and cry. The common strength you draw from friends is invaluable.

9. Uplift your child continually in prayer. Remember God is in charge.

10. Hang a big *spatula* in a prominent place to remind you that your hand and God's are the only ones which can pull you off the emotional ceiling of self-pity.

We Start Where We Are

Again and again, mothers have found in Barbara Johnson a sympathetic, supportive, spiritual, and frankly smiling woman friend.

Barbara confidently and joyfully looks forward to the day when Larry will return to the Lord. For now, God has "healed" *her,* and that is miracle enough to make each day count for *joy.* A glance in her direction might even reveal a *spatula* in her hand, in case there is someone on the ceiling!

Barbara has a few last thoughts of encouragement for parents who are suffering because of their children.

"We cannot tally the final score on a child's life until the game is over. Our children at at halftime and some of them are failing badly. But God can touch their hearts and turn them around.

"If they are Christians, they belong to God. We come to a place as parents where we have to say, 'Whatever, Lord,' instead of 'Why me?'

"The verse which reads, 'The secret things belong to the Lord' (Deut. 29:29) is very obscure but very special to me. There are some things which will never make sense here on earth, and for which we will not find answers.

"As parents we cannot go back and unscramble the eggs. We start where we are and go from there. The past is over like a cancelled check. Tomorrow is a promissory note. Today is cash. Spend it wisely!"

Robbi Kenney of Minneapolis is founder/ director of OUTPOST, a ministry to individuals struggling with homosexuality.

5

Can God Use Me?

An *outpost* may be defined as a security detachment thrown out by a main body of troops to protect it from enemy surprises. When I met Robbi Kenney, I realized that this was a pretty good definition of what her *outpost* is all about. It is a ministry to homosexuals, located in Minneapolis. It hasn't been in existence very long, but Robbi and her co-worker Ed have already earned their right to be heard.

Robbi's Story

When I first began counseling, friends told me I should change my name. Frequently, gay women may pick up a nickname that is unisex or definitely masculine. My friends were afraid I would damage my ministry if I kept "Robbi." However, as it has turned out, the real problem with my name is that people assume that the head of our ministry must be a man; so letters are sent to "Mr. Robbi Kenney, Director."

Robbi is short for Roberta (which no one calls me), and I like the name. I also like being a woman, single, and in a leadership position with a ministry that is as unique as OUTPOST is. We counsel with Christians who have become convinced that their homosexual behavior and lifestyle is sin, and therefore not pleasing to God. They want help breaking their old patterns of behavior and relationships.

What is a 25-year-old woman without a degree in counseling or administration, without formal Bible training, and without a gay testimony doing in a ministry like this?

I think God wanted to make a point, to show the church that believers who have never been gay can help someone who is. And He took a person without any previous understanding of the problem to show that all He needs to accomplish His will is for her to have a willing heart to serve Him, regardless of where that leads.

I am not a feminist. I do what I do because I am willing to serve Jesus, not because I think that women have been downgraded and left out of leadership activities by chauvinistic men. I think my involvement in ministry is a good example of what Paul wrote to the Corinthians: "But God hath chosen the foolish things of the world to confound the wise; and God hath chosen the weak things of the world to confound the things which are mighty" (1 Cor. 1:27, KJV).

Interest Sparked

The ministry's roots go back to my sophomore year in high school. When I was 15, I fell in love with the boy who sat in front of me in homeroom. On the first day of school, I decided that I was going to marry this fellow or die trying! I nearly did. We became good friends and dated off and on throughout high school. But in my senior year, he took another girl to the homecoming game and dance, and that night I drank half a gallon of wine and swallowed 500 aspirins.

But God kept me safe. I lived through the depression of that fall and winter to encounter Christ as my personal Saviour in February of 1972. It changed my life in many ways, but it didn't even touch my feelings for this fellow. I continued to believe that we would get married and live happily ever after. Of course, I began to see that he would have to get saved too, so I began spending a lot of time praying in that direction.

We parted company for a few months as we both headed off for college. But he was back in town about Thanksgiving. Much to my dismay, I found him in the psychiatric unit of the local hospital for what he called an "emotional breakdown." Just before Christmas, he told me he was gay.

When bad things happen to me, I have a coping mechanism—I slip into "automatic pilot." Emotionally, I go blank. My immediate reaction to his news probably appeared to be "Christian." I was calm, loving, and supportive. I told him that it didn't matter, that I would always love him, that our relationship wouldn't be affected.

I didn't collapse until I got home, and then the physical feelings reminded me of falling out of the jungle gym at school when I was little and having the air knocked out of me. First I couldn't breathe, and then I sobbed convulsively. In the midst of the pain, all I could think of was that he needed me now more than ever. Some girls might have looked at the situation and thought, *Okay, we have here first of all a non-Christian who hasn't shown much of an openness to the things of God. On top of that he prefers men to women sexually and emotionally. I think I'll get out while I still have my sanity.* But I was so deeply involved emotionally and had already made him so much a part of my existence, that I just could not let go.

I began to voraciously read everything I could get my hands on that had anything to do with homosexuality. My friend made sure I read books that pointed out the validity of the gay lifestyle. I resisted this kind of thinking, not so much because God called it sin, but because I simply could not accept losing him. I found it equally unbearable knowing that his lifestyle was what *he* wanted. I began to ask myself: *Do I love him enough to let him go and do what is going to make him happy? Yes, of course, I have to. What else can I do? Since I am going to lose him anyway, I should be as gracious as I can about it.*

A Christian Perspective

I had also been reading my Bible, and I found a verse that shocked me at first because of all the "once gay, always gay" material I had been reading. The Apostle Paul said that he knew people who used to be homosexual, but that they weren't anymore! (1 Cor. 6:11) If someone were genuinely willing to commit his life to Christ, a real change in heart and life would take place. I took that to my friend and began badgering him about the fact that he could change if he accepted Christ. No way! He didn't want to change and was very happy doing his thing, thank you very much.

I went to my pastor and asked for counsel, sharing the pain I'd been experiencing. He told me two things: that I should drop the relationship (counsel I had received several times already but wouldn't act on); and that my friend was "beyond hope," because there wasn't anything God could do for a homosexual.

Well, according to *my* Bible, there was lots of hope! And I wasn't going to forsake my friend when he obviously needed *someone* to minister the truth to him. I made another decision not to let go.

The next three years I experienced the grief process of losing this relationship, although I wouldn't admit that I had lost it. I grew stronger in the Lord, in my own personhood, in my belief that God loves homosexuals. And one day, working in a Christian bookstore in Minneapolis, I ran across a newly published book entitled *Gay Liberation* by Roberta Laurila. I read it avidly and wrote the author to share my surprise and admiration, for she confirmed the "theology" that had evolved in my heart regarding homosexuality and God's will. She was a former homosexual, and the book was the description of her deliverance from the bondage of her old gay lifestyle.

About that time another book was published entitled *The Third Sex?* by Kent Philpott. Again, it was a confirmation of my growing thoughts. And again I wrote to the author expressing my joy. Kent passed my letter along to a man he knew who had begun a ministry called *Love in Action.* Brother Frank was also a former homosexual, and his ministry had been organized specifically to help others break free from that sin problem.

Throughout 1975 I wrote many letters to Roberta and to Brother Frank. I poured out my heart regarding my friend. I had hopes for his salvation and our relationship. They both faithfully ministered to me month after month. Soon they felt I would be able to emotionally support several Christians they knew in the Twin Cities area who were breaking out of the gay life. When someone from my area wrote to them after reading their books, they referred the person to me. I was honored, yet afraid. Who was I to be doing this sort of counseling?

During the winter of 1975—76 I "counseled" with people who had been sent to see me, and others who had simply heard about me and had come to the bookstore looking for me. I was leery of billing myself as a counselor, so I tried to become friends with those who came for encouragement or help. At the same time, my work at the bookstore had opened up new vistas for me. Because I had been financially unable to finish at the university in my chosen field of journalism, I believed that I was not qualified to pursue some of my interests. Now I found that I could venture into new areas if I was willing to work. Owning and managing my own bookstore was a dream I nurtured for a while. I also loved children's literature and enjoyed dabbling in writing.

Direction for My Life

But my passion was missions. I gobbled up all the books I could on overseas mission work. In the spring of 1976, I felt God wanted me to offer Him my life as a missionary. I'd been drawn to Ireland for years, because of my own roots there, and because of the conflict in Northern Ireland.

I also felt the need to make a clean break with everything that had *anything* to do with homosexuality and the years of friendship with my gay friend. It just wasn't healthy for me to be dwelling on it any more. I wanted to live an exciting, adventurous life. C.S. Lewis' *The Chronicles of Narnia* showed me a lifestyle I wanted to taste. I fanned the spark of desire for dangerous living such as I read about in Elisabeth Elliot's *Shadow of the Almighty*. I didn't want to live in the past. I wanted to live for Jesus and make every minute count. Too many minutes had passed in devotion to a dead cause.

My way of "getting on with things" was to plan a trip to Ireland to make contacts regarding my future. I made plans to leave in September, and everything was going smoothly. I had the money I needed, my ticket to London and Dublin was paid for, and I was leaving in three days.

Roberta, my author friend, called me unexpectedly at work to tell me she had been invited to attend a conference of ex-gays, men and women who had left the gay life and were interested in ministering to others with the same problem. Since she couldn't get the time off from work, she asked me to take her book and represent her at this conference in Los Angeles. I was incredulous when I discovered the conference began the very day I was to leave for Ireland.

I murmured, "Oh, dear," and tried to explain how God was leading me overseas. I expressed my gratitude for all that she had done for me, but told her, "No." I simply couldn't do it. Before she hung up, Roberta asked me to pray about it. I mechanically told her I would, but I already knew God's mind on this matter, and I wasn't going to even bring it up with Him!

I spent a miserable three days trying to ignore God. Finally, somewhat grudgingly, I gave in and changed my flight plans. I cried as my plane landed at the Los Angeles International Airport. Little did I know that "LAX" and San Francisco International were going to be familiar stops in the years ahead. The EXIT Summit Conference for ex-gays interested in ministry was held at Melodyland Christian Center, just across the street from Disneyland.

What *was* I doing here? I was confused. Did God want to make me healthy and whole? Dwelling on homosexuality and my emotional wholeness seemed mutually exclusive to me. Meeting Brother Frank and Kent Philpott were high points of the conference. (When Kent later asked me what I foresaw in my future, I told him I believed that I would marry an ex-gay! That's how far I'd come in breaking out of my own mind-set!) It was also a thrill to see 60 men and women (mostly men) meeting each other for the first time, crying and saying to one another, "I thought I was the only one!" This was a new experience for them too. Most had broken from the gay life alone, and had always felt like freaks in comparison to the rest of the church world that seemed so normal and uncomplicated.

I was uncomfortable as I watched and listened for those three days, wondering what God's intentions were. I was a minority in a minority. There was only a handful of women, and of the women I was one of the only "straights." I identified with those interested in ministry, but didn't envision myself becoming deeply involved. Some assumed too that I didn't know much about what was going on because of my heterosexual background. That irritated me, and I was already feeling defensive. I wondered why I had given up Ireland for this.

OUTPOST

Things didn't fall into place until several weeks later. One evening, sitting at home chatting with my roommate, I was idly flipping through the dictionary when I came across the word *outpost*. It read:

outpost/'aut-post/ n la: a security detachment thrown out by a main body of troops to protect it from enemy surprise b: a military base established by treaty or agreement in another country 2a: an outlying frontier settlement b: an outlying branch or position of a main organization or group

Something clicked. I thought, *A frontier fortification against the enemy's sneak attack . . . hmmm. Good name for a ministry. . . .*

And the Lord said, "Yes, *yours!"*

This marked the beginning of OUTPOST. I wish I could say that from then on I yielded myself to Christ as His dutiful servant, forsaking all to follow the road that God had made plain to me. Unfortunately, the grass always did seem greener in Ireland, and I couldn't shake the feeling that ex-gay ministry was too offbeat for me since I did not come from that background. I was quizzed about my past and about my former dream of marrying my old friend. I was accused of ministering out of my need, not by direction of the Lord; or of being a "fruit fly" (a straight woman who hangs around gay men and gay bars because she's afraid of contact with heterosexual men). Even ex-gay friends in ministry sometimes questioned my motivation. At times it hardly seemed worth the effort. Overseas mission work is so much more respectable.

But my ministry involvement grew quickly. I was the only available counselor in the Midwest, and I received many referrals. My growing counseling load began to keep me busy every night after work. I felt that I had no time for myself. Wasn't there *anyone* else in my area with a similar burden, someone to consult with about these unique problems?

It was with a giant sigh of relief that I found a seminar entitled "Christian and Gay?" to be held one afternoon on the university campus. I arrived in great anticipation, my Bible under my arm. I noted, with some consternation, that I was the only one with a Bible, and was afraid that I had stumbled into the wrong room or had gotten the dates mixed up.

But I was in the right place. A young priest came in with a file folder, sat down, and opened the discussion with a remark about homosexuality. Almost immediately, I realized why there were no Bibles. These were Roman Catholics who believed God had made them gay. It was a Dignity meeting. They were quite upset with me when I read Romans 1:26-27 and 1 Corinthians 6:11 to them. Mostly I listened quietly. But afterward the priest exploded in anger at me. He waved his file folder saying that "years of research" had shown that people cannot change, and he stalked out.

But one man in the group said he'd like to talk with me. He had a saving knowledge of Jesus. God had convicted him that his gay behavior was sin, and he wanted help dealing with it. This was the first time he'd ever heard the biblical viewpoint about turning from homosexuality. I didn't find help for me, but the need for the ministry was confirmed.

In 1977 I tried to go to Ireland again. Plans were cut right off when the sponsors of the Anaheim conference invited me to the second national conference to be held in June in Oakland, California. They asked me to share my "expertise" at being a non-gay in ministry to gays and ex-gays. I agreed, knowing full well that the only "expertise" I had was in trying to run from the Lord!

But something else happened to cut short my wandering thoughts. Dan Morstad, the director of a local Christian hotline, had heard about me. He wanted someone to do the follow-up work on the Love Lines calls dealing with homosexuality. He asked if I would present OUTPOST to his board of directors. It sounded as if this might solve some of my problems! I worked out of a big cardboard box "office" and had done my counseling in local restaurants. To expand the ministry, I needed a base of operations. This Christian hotline looked like just the thing.

Within the next few days, I lost my job in the bookstore, though the manager gave me one month's salary for severance pay. This should have been a traumatic event, but it did not shake me as much as I expected.

I almost forgot about it the next day in my excitement at going before the Love Lines board to present the ministry. They received me enthusiastically and voted me on the Love Lines staff at the meeting. I shared my need for a job with them and they prayed with me. The next day one of the board members arranged a job interview and I was working again by the end of the week!

Within the next six months I decided to go full time with OUTPOST. The counseling workload was increasing and I was receiving more out-of-state letters requesting information and litera-ture. The Love Lines staff were getting more calls from men and women who were tired of the gay life and wanted a way out. And at the second national conference in Oakland, I had been appointed to the board of directors for the national "umbrella" organization EXODUS International that serves as a communication network for involved ex-gay ministries.

Can God Use Me?

But I struggled with my self-worth. My assets were that I was a single woman from a never-been-gay background. I brought a perspective to ministering that ex-gay counselors couldn't bring, particularly in not viewing homosexuality as the worst and the only sin God abhors. Counselees struggle with the idea that they are worse than other sinners because of this particular sin, and that they are too different to be helped. In my own life I had dealt with pride, unforgiveness, sexual temptation, and sin from which I drew parallels to show that they weren't especially different, let alone unreachable.

I knew that I was performing a service that was publicly

unprecedented in the Twin Cities. *I* was the one who answered the phone calls and *I* gave the help. It was *I* who presented seminars in churches. Even though I couldn't identify exactly with their experiences, the men seeking counsel never refused to sit and talk with me. They were willing to hear the truth from anyone who was willing to share it. Yes, I *knew* I was being used intellectually. But it wasn't heart knowledge.

At home by myself or with my roommate, I would beseech God for wisdom and discernment, for right words and right attitudes. I lived in fear that I would get in God's way and hamper His work.

There is a godly fear that is good and keeps us alive to the conviction of the Holy Spirit. But there is a type of self-consciousness that is not of God. It's a reverse kind of pride that says, "God, You really don't know what You're doing. I'm no good, I'm not worthy of Your love, I am incapable of doing Your work." This is sin. How dare we tell the Creator that we are exempt from His working all things for good in our lives according to His purpose? (See Romans 8:28.) When I understood this, I began walking in freedom, knowing that the Lord was working in and through me. I just had to be available. At times I succumbed to this negative attitude again, but I learned to recognize my Enemy, and not to be caught for long in this trap.

I turned my attention next to another problem. Though I spent 18-hour days in the office, I could not get to the important things, like developing literature and training materials. I was swamped with the "busy work" that never seemed to get finished.

My Anaheim friends recommended a two-day seminar put on by World Vision called "Managing Your Time." My attendance there was probably the single most important thing I ever did for OUTPOST. When I returned I had in my possession a complete set of ministry objectives and steps to achieve each practical goal I, myself, had set. I also had the plans for a filing system that was a headache to set up but a real boon in the long run. And in the process, I discovered my spiritual gift of "governments" or administrative capability.

OUTPOST Staff

That winter a man that I had counseled was laid off his job because of a physical disability. He had developed a deep spiritual quality, and his eagerness to help me was so convincing that I decided I could risk having him do some office and phone work. I had the services of three women friends who were willing to counsel with me, so God actually brought together a staff for OUTPOST before I had a chance to think much about it.

I still felt, though, that I needed a solid ex-gay man to work with me—someone who had been out of the lifestyle for some time and could look back and see the growth in his own life as he submitted to Christ. There was an unfinished feel to OUTPOST. I began praying about this need.

I had met several men at the Oakland conference, and began corresponding with one in particular. Ed Hurst was the leader of the evangelistic effort at Christ for the Nations Institute in Dallas that was called the Outreach to Gay Areas. He had a real flair for expressing himself in his letters, and it made me think that anything he put his hand to would probably find its way into print.

I had a growing conviction that Ed should join us at OUTPOST and one night on the phone he agreed that he had been thinking this too. He began right after graduation from Bible school.

OUTPOST has been blessed with one of the most articulate men in the ex-gay movement. From Ed's letters I pieced together a testimony that was printed in *Christian Life* magazine the summer of 1978. His testimony and his teachings on the roots of homosexuality have become the backbone of our literature department. Together Ed and I have taught seminars for the Lutheran Conference on the Holy Spirit, the national convention for the Christian Association for Psychological Studies, and our own conference in the Midwest that drew people interested in this ministry from as far away as Vermont and Alabama.

Today OUTPOST offers counseling based on the Word of God to individuals struggling with homosexuality, as well as other sexual problems (and to parents, spouses, or friends). We produce a free monthly newsletter, conduct seminars, and send speaking teams to churches and other groups.

OUTPOST is committed to three things: (1) educating the church to its responsibility and capability of ministering to a group of people largely ignored due to the nature of their sin; (2) discipling believers in such a way that they can walk in freedom given to them at salvation as new creatures in Christ, over all areas of sin, but particularly homosexuality; and (3) evangelizing the gay community with the Good News of Jesus Christ and the message of freedom from gayness possible to those who make Christ their Lord.

I delight in looking back and seeing God's progression in my life. I was confused and cynical at that first meeting, feeling like a nobody and wishing I were someplace else. God has changed me into a ministry leader, succeeding in a major undertaking, confident of being in the right place at the right time for God's purpose.

What Can You Do?

There are several things you can do, if you think God is calling you to have a ministry to homosexuals.

1. Be available. Tell your pastor you are open to befriending people from gay backgrounds who want counsel. Open your home to them once a week for dinner. Or be willing to have them move in with you as they complete their break from their past lives. Many times hurting believers actually need re-parenting. They need to relate to a family that loves and accepts them—something they may never have had themselves.

2. Be familiar with the available literature on helping those from gay backgrounds. You may not become involved with an ongoing ministry to gays, but some people you know—probably in your own church—may be in need of these encouraging words: that there is hope of dealing with this sin problem; that God loves homosexuals. Hurting people silently study the Christians around them, never revealing themselves. They watch for accepting attitudes because they don't want to be hurt. They are aware of those who only perceive the problem of homosexuality as a political issue and do not see them as hurting people. But they will go to a person who has demonstrated through his conversation real compassion for those coming from gay backgrounds.

3. Rent a post office box and run an ad in the local paper saying you'd be willing to correspond with all who are troubled by their gayness and want to know how Jesus can help them. Assure them of confidentiality. This is particularly vital in small towns.

4. Invest some money in literature to put into the hands of pastors in your town. The booklet "Healing for the Homosexual," published by the Presbyterian Charismatic Communion, is especially good for this use because it is so well-rounded in the type of information it includes. (It also has a referral list for ex-gay ministries that includes OUTPOST!)

5. Take a friend and hit the streets! Share the Gospel near those places that are known for being "gay." You needn't major on homosexuality. Just let those you talk with know that Jesus can

change their lives even if they are gay. Don't be limited by the men's gay scene. Search out where the lesbian community gathers, go and be a friend.

6. If you don't feel that any of the above are "you," support your nearest ex-gay ministry financially, prayerfully, and by volunteering your services. Most ministries are in dire need of secretaries, bookkeepers, fund raisers, etc. Your talents for organization, good financial stewardship, or public relations are very much needed.

Dawn Menning is the wife of Minnesota state senator Mike Menning, and mother of two sons. She is a former elementary school teacher.

6
Patterning for Tomorrow

Anita Bryant tells how in the thick of the controversy regarding the Dade County (Florida) homosexual rights, Minnesota State Senator Marion (Mike) Menning—as well as other legislators across the country—came to support her.

"We heard from senators and state representatives from almost every state in the country. Typical of their comments are these: Senator Marion Menning, who led the successful fight in Minnesota against the state's 'special privileges' law, stated, 'It's a threat to my personal rights; it's a threat to my religious beliefs'" *(The Anita Bryant Story,* Revell, 1977).

Mike is a farmer from southwest Minnesota. Mike and his wife, Dawn, are the parents of two boys. God has used both Mike and Dawn in uniquely different ways in their desire to serve God, their country, and their community.

Young Senator Menning has earned a reputation for his solid Christian commitment as well as his courage to speak out on issues that are threatening a free society.

But this is Dawn Menning's story and seated in his office at the state capitol, Mike glows with pride as he speaks of his wife—a loving mother, and a woman of deep faith in God. When their younger son was born, and through the first months of his life, they hoped that he would become a strong, healthy playmate for his brother. When the Mennings took Michael in for his two-year-old checkup, he was diagnosed as *microcephalic* (a word they couldn't even define). Michael has needed constant care, and Dawn has welcomed over 50 women from their community into her home to help with the therapy program. While the politician husband and father "works," Dawn and Michael—with older brother Mitchell—follow a regimen that none would have chosen, but all accept! This family has influenced their town of Edgerton.

Dawn's Story

Early on a cold, snowy, Minnesota winter morning on January 18, 1947, I was born to loving parents, and a caring Christian community of 1,000 residents. I grew up as a farmer's daughter who enjoyed life in that role. At just 15 years, I stumbled into a budding romance with a young man who is now my husband, Marion (Mike) Menning. After high school graduation, I attended Dordt College for two years, and then I was hired to teach at my grade school alma mater.

After six years of courtship, Mike and I knew the Lord was directing us to be married. On our wedding night in 1968, as we were driving to the hotel about 50 miles from our hometown, Mike shared with me a dream he wanted to fulfill in our married life. "I'm interested in politics and intend to get more involved someday." I passed it off flippantly, not imagining what God had in store for us!

Entering Politics

I taught school for four more years and continued an effort to complete my college degree—an extra incentive came when Mike started college. After all, I couldn't be left behind in the dust. The spring I resigned my teaching job, Mike announced that he was running for state representative. My intention had been to resign from teaching, finish college, and fulfill my real life's ambition to "be a mother and wife." However, it looked as if the Lord had something else in mind for us. After much prayer, discussion, and encouragement from people, Mike was off and running. I felt scared—could this be God's will for us?

Many party regulars who had encouraged Mike to run soon fell by the wayside when it came to footwork, so Mike and I were really in the race together. I knocked on many, many doors, knowing very well that our opponent's name was a household word and ours was like a foreign language outside of our own community. Finally, Election Day came. The polls closed and God held up a clear sign—not now! We lost. The only happy news of the election night was our announcement that I was expecting!

We picked up the pieces quickly and carried on—hurt, of course. In fact, we were crushed. We had thought this was what God wanted for us, but we kind of decided then that running for office had only served as a "tremendous experience." Since we had been soundly defeated, I thought it would only be a once-in-a-lifetime event.

Before long, though, I began to realize by reading between the lines that Mike felt the campaign had been a building-block experience. But I hoped that time and a new baby at home might change his attitude.

On May 9, 1973 we were blessed with our first son, Mitchell Dean, born during the height of the Watergate scandal. We were thrilled with him and still like the name.

Mike had started a business selling commercial cleaning chemicals to large firms—restaurants, hotels, and factories. Our life seemed quite solid and smooth.

A Second Time

I saw Mike's deep concern for our country and discontentment with things as they were. I had no choice but to agree that the best way to change things was to get involved. But so involved? We were running again, against the same incumbent, for the same office. By then we had built up a better base of support, and we had good name identification. We trusted God for much.

The campaign was tough work now with a toddler to care for. I was somewhat limited in my involvement, but I aimed for three days a week to help knock on doors.

Election Day again. That historic night we had two happy announcements. The one for all the world to know—we had won by a very slim margin, 115 votes; the other, kept to ourselves—I was expecting again.

Now decisions had to move quickly. We had a whole new lifestyle ahead of us! Since Mitchell and I were not tied down for any reason, we decided to move to St. Paul with Mike during the legislative session. That could be a book in itself—city life for a country girl, the big blizzard, the social functions of wives and more.

I must admit that I was beginning to like Mike in his role, especially as I saw that he was extremely happy with his work.

Enlarged Family

On July 2, 1975 we were blessed with another son, Michael Dale. We had prayed for another boy to give Mitchell companionship.

The next four and one-half years of that baby's life would fill volumes with words and tears. I watched Michael's development and quickly stopped comparing him with children his age. He was simply not doing things on schedule. We observed his delayed development and lack of awareness in his world.

Never once has my love for Michael been different than my love for Mitchell. Both are my sons, my charges from God to love and prepare for a lifetime ahead. In Mitchell's case, I share that responsibility with his teachers and I know he'll make it with a firm background for his life. However, it soon became apparent to Mike and me that if we wanted the same groundwork laid for Michael, things were going to have to be different.

On a memorable day in July 1977, we took Michael to be examined for his two-year-old checkup. Now his behavior that day was the same as it was most of the time—he was docile, "very good," and dull. However, a label emerged on that day which supposedly would change his life. At that office visit, our pediatrician diagnosed him as *microcephalic,* simply meaning "small-headed." Also his brain was smaller than it should be.

On our way home that day, Mike and I discussed Michael's future. We knew he was the same boy we had taken into the office, but felt that somehow our doubts were supposed to be quieted with the diagnostic label he now had. Even though the doctor's advice was "Wait and See!" we knew that this was poor advice, since we had already seen our son falling farther and farther behind other children. If he was going to make it, he'd need a super amount of stimulation.

We started praying fervently! "God, open the right doors. We praise You!" Now, that's the tough one for some to understand—*praise.* Yes, God had given us Michael for a purpose, just as He had given us Mitchell. Even though he was now labeled differently, this didn't change our attitude or responsibility toward him. As Christian parents we are commissioned to train up our children. For us, that means Michael too. We just had to find the right tools to accomplish this task.

Therapy Begins

God opened Mike's office door to the right people at the right time—people who offered suggestions and information about Michael's condition. After we read more about work being done with brain-injured children, we were sure that Michael fit into this category. We made the necessary applications for entry to the Institute for the Achievement of Human Potential at Philadelphia, Pennsylvania, and started praying about what to do in the meantime. We decided to enroll Michael in a school situation to stimulate brain activity. That meant transporting him 30 miles away. It also meant that the boys and I would not be returning to St. Paul with Mike in January.

Yes, we had survived another election. In fact, God had led Mike to run for the Minnesota Senate that time and with some hesitation, I had agreed. We had won with a satisfactory margin.

My primary interest was now centering on Michael. I knew that Mike's close walk with God could allow that. Yet it wasn't easy that January as Mike went 225 miles north, and I drove daily 30 miles south to take Michael to a developmental achievement center. Often as I drove our four-wheel drive truck over Minnesota winter conditions, I wrestled with our problem and asked myself, "Why me?" But God clearly answered, "Why not you?"

That's when I really came to terms with myself and the life God had planned for me. What was so special about me to put me above this kind of thing? I was able, physically and mentally, to cope with this—not alone, but if I let God do the "driving."

God drove us at a much quicker speed than we expected. He seemed to send a bolt of lightning to Mike, striking him with a conviction about building another part of the wall. He was to run for the U.S. Senate. That was a toughy for me. I thought we'd had enough, but Mike was convinced, and I knew God wasn't kidding him. We jumped in with both feet and began the work of campaign preparations. We felt comfortable with how our "building" was progressing until April 1978. We received word that because of a cancellation appointment, we could take Michael for our first meeting with the Institute staff in Philadelphia. While this meant the end of Mike's U.S. Senate pursuit, we had renewed hope and confidence that this was God's method of working a miracle with our son. It wasn't going to be a sudden miracle. It would take much, much concentrated effort on the part of our whole family, and even our community.

A Common Goal

What follows is a story of "When One Finger Hurts." One member of our family was hurt, and it hurt our whole family so badly that we were not going to be satisfied until we had that "hurt" fixed.

We set up a dawn-to-dust schedule of care for Michael. The only relief I found was when Mike took over. We needed 12 volunteers per day at first, and soon had these by asking our community for help. We found that basically, people are caring and sharing, but they need an invitation to help.

We had made sizable changes to accommodate Michael's routine and had to reevaluate our own lives. We also had to assess our activities, asking ourselves which could remain and which enjoyable things had to be discontinued. Often only one of us could attend "couples" events—a tough role at times, but not impossible.

We were now beyond the point of turning back. We knew about this program, believed God had led us to it, and felt He would use it for Michael's good. When I was tempted to fret and worry, I would think deep down, *Worry is like a rocking chair. It occupies your mind, but doesn't get you anywhere!* Concerned about the program and about my being away from Mike, I was given wise counsel from a fellow Christian named Hansi: "Don't dwell on it. In fact, pray that God won't give you time to think about it." I guess that's what happened. My mind was occupied with snow, bad roads, and trucking my volunteers to and from our country home so that they could carry on our patterning program. Many lonely hours were filled with preparations for Michael's intelligence program instead of with crafts activities I had previously enjoyed. Now, the neat side. Michael was getting to be one smart boy who now walked and was very alert almost all of the time.

We were happy to see Daddy come back home after the legislative session. With no campaign for the summer, he would be available to assist some of the time.

That brings us to the present. I have an extremely busy daily routine. It begins at 6:30 A.M., goes straight through until evening dinner at 6 o'clock, and resumes from 7:45 to about 9 P.M. I'm often asked, "How?" My only answer is, "What are my alternatives?" I have taken my role of motherhood seriously because I know this is what God expects. I see good things happening, so I feel pressed on toward a higher goal. Michael doesn't talk yet, so I make the noise in our house. And I have plenty of quiet time to pray, a necessary part of every day to pull me through. We pray daily that Michael's legs will firm up and that he will be able to speak. I am also confident of the prayer support of many Christians who know about our situation. Mike has had opportunities to tell our story to hundreds of Christians and to ask for their support for him, his sons, and me.

Where does Mitchell fit into all of this? He is a well-behaved able-minded, strong-bodied first-grader who loves school, hates bad grades, and adores his brother. He knows he wouldn't want us to stop one part of the patterning program, in case that might be the part needed to fix Michael's brain. He too lives close to Jesus and prays earnestly for the needs of God's people.

Spiritual Growth

How about my future? I can't see what tomorrow will bring here on earth, but one thing is certain. I'm confident that God will supply me grace for *each* day—not for a year, or a session, or a campaign, but for a day. Sometimes I lean on Him to give grace just for that moment.

I'm convinced now, more than ever, that as a child must develop along certain lines, so we must also pattern our lives after God. We crawl before God's throne, lie helpless, and He lifts us up and helps us creep along as weak, growing Christians. He then supplies us with a language of praise in return for what He does for us and lets us walk with Him. That doesn't mean we'll never stumble and land right back on our bellies crawling again, but that God is available to help us in His special way through those times. The following story describes God's special way of helping us.

One Night I Had a Dream . . .

I dreamed I was walking along the beach with the Lord, and across the sky flashed scenes from my life. For each scene I noted two sets of footprints in the sand. One set belonged to me, the other to the Lord.

When the last scene of my life flashed before me I looked back at the footprints in the sand. I noticed that many times along the path of my life, there was only one set of footprints. I also noticed that it happened at the very lowest and saddest times in my life.

I questioned the Lord about it. "Lord, You said that once I decided to follow You, You would walk with me all the way, but I notice that during the most troublesome times in my life, there is only one set of footprints. I don't understand why in times when I needed You most, You would leave."

The Lord replied, "My precious child, I would never leave you during your times of trial and suffering. When you see only one set of footprints, it was then that I carried you."

Author Unknown

A Future Together

Right now the role of motherhood nearly overwhelms me. I'm here at home while Mike's work is with issues, people, and problems of our state. His acquaintances are political and spiritual and special. Mine are Michael's patterns, relatives, and a rather new group of friends from our local Christian Women's Club. Mike has big opportunities to witness, engage in floor fights on moral issues, and give testimonies in churches. My activities are pretty much the same from day to day. The spirit of jealousy has been my greatest enemy and I must often fight it away. Mike and I strive hard to keep our lines of communication wide open. One way we do this is by praying honestly together.

Mike's deep concern for the future of our country is also mine. I'm convinced that Christians must wake up, pray, and WORK! Much good and motivational literature is being written by Christians. I do make time to read, because it help me so much. However, some of the books make me feel miserable—when I read how God has worked quick miracles for some of His people. He is putting us through a slower process. It is then that I need to be reminded of God's mysterious ways.

Mike and I want to face our future together. We also want to follow God's direction and to fulfill our responsibility as parents. I must trust God to show me the way, His way, to be faithful as mother—and wife.

Building Blocks You Can Place

Pornography

1. Refuse to shop where pornography is sold, and be sure to let the proprietor know why you are not patronizing his business.

2. Become informed about pornography in your area and throughout the country. For example, subscribe to the *Morality in Media* newsletter.

3. Read books such as *How to Stop the Porno Plague.*

4. Consider "browsing" in an adult bookstore. About 50 women in Minneapolis are using this technique. A group of five or six women arrive, unannounced, greet people at the door, stand behind customers, watch those viewing movies, and generally make their presence felt, hoping this will drive customers away.

5. Additional resources:
   Citizens for Decency through Law, 450 Leader Building, Cleveland, Ohio 44114.
   Morality in Media, 475 Riverside Drive, New York, New York 10027.

Homosexuality

1. Follow the suggestions regarding ministry to gays listed in chapters 4 and 5.

2. Support Christian ex-gay ministries—financially, prayerfully, and with your volunteer work.

3. Additional resources:
   OUTPOST, 328 E. Hennepin Ave., Minneapolis, Minnesota 55414.

Spatula Ministries, Box 444, LaHabra, California 90631.
(Literature and cassette tapes are available.)
Love in Action (Frank Worthen), P.O. Box 2655, San
Rafael, California 94902.
Vision Ministries (Roberta Laurila), P.O. Box 1179,
Grand Rapids, Michigan 49504.
Committee on Moral Concerns, P.O. Box 20096, Sacra-
mento, California 95820.

Personal Crisis
1. Consider how you can tangibly help people who are faced
with personal crises in their lives.
2. Investigate what your church could do, through existing
organizations or by initiating new programs.
3. Seek assistance from appropriate county, state, or federal
agencies.

SECTION II

WHO IS YOUR NEIGHBOR?

KAYDI LARSON, using her home for retreats, reaches out to those in need.

IRIS FULCHER uses the potential of Religious Release Time classes in the public school to reach children for Christ.

BETTY BOTTOMLY shows compassion learned as a military wife to the many who come to their ranch ministry.

MALETTOR CROSS ministers with her husband through an inner-city mission.

ELEANOR SAMS, editor of a community current events newsletter, shares much-needed information with her neighbors.

Nehemiah said, "Go, eat the fat, drink the sweet, and give a part to him for whom nothing is prepared; for this is a holy day to our Lord. Do not grieve, for the joy of the Lord is your strength." Nehemiah 8:10, BERK

Kaydi Larson lives with her husband and family in the woods of Minnesota, where they conduct retreat ministries. A grandmother with a talent in furniture refinishing, she is interested in antiques, and is an accomplished artist.

7
Disciple to the Disadvantaged

How many times have I tried to describe Kaydi to someone? She is indescribable—probably my most unique friend. In *The Sound of Music* the song questions, "How do you find a word that means Maria? A flibbertijibbet! A will-o-the-wisp! A clown!" It asks, "How do you keep a wave upon the sand?" and "How do you catch a moonbeam in your hand?"

Kaydi is both elusive and determined. Kaydi has had a varied career, including a brief time spent in South America.

Kaydi personifies the gift of compassion. She is an artist, and her beautiful frugality, her appreciation of old things, fine furniture, and flowers, all reveal her unique *gifts*.

Kaydi is incredible, and it pleasures me to introduce her to you. God has built Christian character in her life, and her days and weeks now are spent in building an actual house to His glory.

Kaydi Tells Her Story
"She's dead. She died this morning of a cerebral hemorrhage. There was nothing I could do." The grieving husband turned to the chipped cement steps leading up to the tiny back porch.

I was speechless. I muttered something about my willingness to help with his children—anytime. That day and in the weeks that followed, I was strangely silent. I always think better when I don't talk, especially in my relationship with the heavenly Father. He was talking now, and it was if I could audibly hear the accusing words: *Unconcerned. Uninvolved. Unconcerned. Uninvolved!*

My neighbor had been in her early 30s, as I was, and five children were now motherless. She had been an untiring worker. In addition to maternal duties, she had worked the afternoon-evening shift as a downtown waitress. She had wanted to be my friend, but a number of things had made that impossible: the formidable hedge, my aloof personality, and my demanding schedule.

Rather than conversing through a prickly maze of buckthorn, she would walk around to my front steps, having hung out her interminable load of wash. In our seasoned geographical location, I was never sure if we lived in an upper-lower-class neighborhood or a lower-middle-class one. If one did *not* have a dryer, perhaps one lived in the lower-class. (And of course, I had a dryer.)

Not My Type

She just wasn't my type of person. Along with an occasional bit of profanity, she had a nasal Brooklyn accent. And she smoked! Imagine! No doubt, that was the main reason I never invited her into my house. Besides smoking, and not having a dryer, she worked *outside* the home, indicating that she was dissatisfied either with her fulfilling happy-home situation or with her husband's economic contribution.

Unconcerned. Uninvolved. Unconcerned. Uninvolved. I began to weep. The tears were hot with shame and contrition, as I wished that she could come back so I could be the friend for whom she had been looking. But it was too late. All the spaghetti casseroles I sent to this motherless family the following year did not erase the memory of my arrogance.

Surely I had all the friends I could possibly need—nice, proper, Christian friends who rarely did anything unconventional. They taught Sunday School, enjoyed family picnics, and attended church regularly. I really didn't know anyone who cultivated the habit of collecting assorted friends (especially ones who couldn't afford a dryer)—except Jesus.

Tears of accusation crowded my eyes again. What she had wanted most from me, I had refused to give her. My separatism had successfully blockaded the loving flow of sharing friendship that God had intended for both of our lives.

Besides not wanting any new friends, I had been too busy. The list of priorities was long and suddenly unimpressive. I had wrapped my entire life around my family and friends, creating an artistic, colorful atmosphere of enjoyment for them.

You Must Be Kidding!

Considering myself deservedly chastened, I yearned to demonstrate Christian love to others. I asked my patient heavenly Father what I should do. *Where should I start? In my own neighborhood? You must be kidding, God! OK . . .*

I prayed as I walked down the alley to the home of my youngest daughter's small friend. Would this mother think I was weird? As it turned out I discovered a new friend who was hungry for a women's sharing group. *God is so good!*

Together we plotted our strategy. We invited neighborhood women in a two-block radius, by personal contact or written invitation. Most of them refused to believe that we were not selling jewelry, laundry powder, or plastic strainers. That evening, 25 ladies filled my living room. We shared our plan for a neighbor sharing-study group, and we set the starting date. Half of them came on a regular, weekly basis for over seven years!

Coming from all backgrounds and denominational preferences, we found a unity in the redeeming Person of Jesus Christ. I particularly remember two women from those Thursday evenings: an aging but indestructible Grandma Irene, who trimmed tall trees regularly; and Mary, a weary mother who had raised seven children in a neighborhood that often, justifiably, did not appreciate children in large numbers. Mary's first husband had left her but her second marriage was, in comparison, more peaceful and secure. Nevertheless, Mary was still a social outcast until Grandma Irene brought her one night. Mary soon became verbally excited about her trust in God.

But years and leukemia move too quickly. Although still in her early 50s, Mary seemed to sense that her earthly pilgrimage was over. Several of our women were with her the evening in the hospital when she told her gathered children about her acquaintance with Jesus and her joyful expectation of seeing Him soon! A few hours later Mary departed, nonstop, to heaven's resting place.

Everyone in our study group missed Mary; Grandma Irene mourned her passing. From them both I learned lessons I shall never forget. For me, the hobby of friend-collecting was still new. Grandma Irene had shown all of us how to do it God's way. In the midst of Christian neighbors, she *alone* had literally loved Mary into a relationship where Mary dared to join our little group, assured that she would feel the continuation of Grandma's God-given affection. She found there the acceptance and friendship which transformed her last years. And for me, there would be other "Marys."

Three Heart Attacks

Prior to this new direction in my life, my husband had resigned from the sales jungle. The visible approval of the heavenly Father had come in the form of a vacant hardware store, destined to become our antique shop and refinishing studio for the next decade.

We opened with an enormous three-piece mahogany bedroom set to refinish. A few weeks later my husband's first heart attack occurred. There were two more in the next five years. In each traumatic scene, complete with ambulance siren, our loving Lord surrounded us and our three children with fantastic peace, employee assistance, and sufficient funds to satisfy the hospital business office. (No longer was there that marvelous company hospitalization on which to rely.) I was forced to trust God in a new way; and although a life of financial faith is exciting, and I cherish those years that taught us so much together about heavenly insurance, I found it difficult. I have always been able to trust God for anything—except money!

One day when we had no money to pay the shop rent, a lady came rushing in and purchased the hand-painted desk in the window. It was exactly the amount due our patient landlord! Oddly enough, I, who once had criticized mothers working outside the home, found myself joining the club, without a guilt complex.

New Directions

Ten incredible years chugged past. Our little studio required much tedious handwork; we could never afford or discover enough laborers to expand sufficiently. My perceptive husband sensed that God had something different in mind for us. Typically, I balked. "We'll add a boutique line," I offered. And I began to design children's clothing, toys, and sundries.

My mind was changed after an automobile accident in which my car was struck from behind by a car going 30 miles an hour. The driver had been late for work; in addition, he now had totaled his auto! I had been driving an indestructible 1966 Chevy and the sustained injuries to my chassis were minor. God was very gracious to me that day. I also felt He was reinforcing my husband's decision to close the studio and was turning me in another direction.

At this time, I was teaching an adult Sunday School class in a neighborhood church. During church one Sunday morning, the Holy Spirit suggested very emphatically that I speak to the young woman in front of me. When the service was over, I introduced myself and found Marcia enthusiastically seizing my offered friendship.

Marcia was my first contact with the world of welfare, which I have often referred to as a "fourth-world country." As our family became involved with her family of four offspring, we learned of her recent acquaintance with Jesus Christ, her dismal past, her unsuccessful marriages, her triumph over alcoholism, and her present struggle as a student at the university.

Often I wondered if I would have been able to endure what she did during those years of academic pressures, maternal responsibilities and never-ending financial squeezes. I doubt that many of us who critically view the welfare recipients from the grocery check-out line could successfully survive on their allowances from month to month. Marcia faced not only the humiliation of food stamps, but also the incessant red tape involved when the plumbing pipes popped, an ambulance was needed, or the harassment of a neighbor necessitated legal assistance.

What Can I Do?

For Marcia and for those women on the outside of our secure Christian society, I began to ache. *Dear God, what can I do?*

My own life was compounded by physical problems—an early menopause, and a chemical addiction to Valium as a result of the accident. I prayed as I had done so often: "Father, dear, I'm a mess. I need some verses!" And He answered with Isaiah 58:7-11 (LB):

I want you to share your food with the hungry and bring right into your own homes those who are helpless, poor, and destitute. Clothe those who are cold and don't hide from relatives who need your help. If you do these things, God will shed His own glorious light upon you. He will heal you; your godliness will lead you forward, and goodness will be a shield before you, and the glory of the Lord will protect you from behind. Then, when you call, the Lord will answer. "Yes, I am here," He will quickly reply. All you need to do is to stop oppressing the weak, and to stop making false accusations and spreading vicious rumors!

Feed the hungry! Help those in trouble! Then your light will shine out from the darkness, and the darkness around you shall be as bright as day. And the Lord will guide you continually, and satisfy you with all good things, and keep you healthy too; and you will be like a well-watered garden, like an ever-flowing spring.

I took these promises very personally. If I would reach out to the oppressed, God would heal me. And He did. For the rest of my transitory life, I shall claim these verses.

A hysterectomy followed for a condition which might have been malignant but was not; miraculously it also solved one of my most debilitating difficulties.

Six months later, I was asked to teach the Bible study at a large downtown church which had an established, exciting, weekly ministry with inner-city women. Was I ready? *God, how good You are! I adore You!* But I was apprehensive.

The group consisted mostly of white women with some American Indian women, but all were from the fourth-world country of welfare; all were under the pressure of problems beyond my comprehension. How patient they were with me during those years. Each week I plowed through Scripture, verse by verse (as we had in our neighborhood group) for 45 minutes, until most of them were almost asleep. One day, a dear co-worker suggested that we begin using a booklet with fill-in blanks. Most of the women could read and write. We took half a lesson each time; and though it was tedious, they found new freedom in expressing and sharing their needs because they were individually involved in thinking and writing.

I learned to appreciate using a simple translation of the Bible—in newspaper language—and referred to the verses by page number rather than by book title. Often I was the one who learned the most during those unforgettable years.

One of the women that God used in my life was an American Indian mother of 13 children, raising two grandbabies. By keeping in touch with this woman and her brood, I was providentially led into the north area of our city, where the crime rate was the highest and the income the lowest. This was my first glimpse of our city's minorities.

It happened on a summer Sunday morning, when my daughter, a

high school senior, was traveling with me. We were looking for a local mission where she wanted to test-teach a class of inner-city youngsters, as a means to help her decide on a college major. Finding the mission locked, we retreated to a supermarket parking lot to think. Suddenly, I remembered my native American friend and the neighborhood church her children attended; so we headed for north Minneapolis.

The atmosphere hummed with exuberant chaos and warmth as blacks, whites, and native Americans found their places in the small chapel. My special friend's youngest five were in the front row. The service was geared to the needs of the people and I was impressed with the opportunity for the congregation to voice their prayer requests. Audible intercession followed: for the sick, for someone behind bars, for landlord difficulties, and for diverse necessities. Without any difficulty, my daughter and I each acquired a Sunday School class.

Initially, my husband voiced apprehension at our activity in this questionable location, but his attitude soon became one of support and encouragement. For the first time as a family, we began to ponder the problems of minority, inner-city people: the frustration of jobless men, the dismal perspective of the women, the suspicion of even the preschooler. To this segment of humanity, the city had allotted a geographical location of crowded housing projects where conditions often erupted into violent and murderous behavior, much of which never reached the daily newspaper.

I cried a lot. The young woman who worked at the church told me that she had cried most of her first week there. Then she had asked God to toughen her emotionally and give her faith and fortitude. The positive, persistent attitude of the energetic, young white pastor was a continual source of inspiration. He had more reasons for discouragement than encouragement: Situations always seemed to reach him in crisis proportions. His parish included the courts, the jails, the restless streets, the housing projects, and the local funeral parlor.

Prior to this new venture, I had been introduced to *Life with Spice* and its creator, the inimitable Daisy Hepburn. I became its enthusiastic illustrator. I also became convinced of its philosophy of involvement—from the opening game or exercise routine to the applicable lesson with sharing time and correlated craft, designed to reinforce God's love for each one as a woman.

It was not difficult to envision using *Life with Spice* with our women every Monday in the little church. For the girls we began a program on Saturdays, bringing them to my home for Girls' Spice. One Saturday was for the first through fourth graders. The alternate Saturday was for fifth grade through junior high. For two and one-half years we ran these programs 12 months a year for women and girls, spending our summers at the church or park with the youngsters and the inevitable games of kickball. God brought marvelous volunteer women and girls to assist with the nursery, transportation, meals, and activities. It was wild and wonderful. In my lily-white neighborhood, the only remark that I ever encountered was: "My, but they are *black!*"

Although I could not live in the community as did the dedicated church staff, I soon began to share the local fears and frustrations as I walked through the neighborhood and spent time in the homes. These people were willing to love and trust me. Never once did I feel that I was discriminated against because I was white. I became impressed with how black people have been at the bottom socially because of their skin color, even though God has made them beautiful, sensitive, and gifted. To us "white" children of the 1980s, He has given the responsibility of showing them how valuable they are. We can share with them all that we have been given (not earned) because of our white ancestry. They must be given equal opportunities in our country.

As I review my encounter with the "fourth world" I think of the child and woman abuse that is commonplace. Life is riddled with aggravating everyday petty problems, with little hope for betterment. And fear dominates every day—fear of muggings, thefts, raids on apartments, court appearances before an impervious white judge, fears for their young children and for daughters who will be into prostitution by age 12. I remember more sadness from their world than happiness.

To the Woods
And then we moved. At the church I bade farewell to my women and girls. I was abruptly transported from involvement in their world to the role of a female carpenter in the woods, in preparation for future ministries.

In our new location, my husband and I held 50 acres of land in joint ownership with our heavenly Father—virgin woods just 45 minutes from the inner city. We designed plans for a four-story A-frame which eventually could be totally heated by wood and solar energy. It would be a home to accommodate future retreat ministries that the Lord had laid on our hearts.

I had observed over the years what a change of environment had meant to the inner-city women—even for a few hours' time. We knew how significant a day or a weekend of sharing and growing in Jesus could be. We wanted to teach mending and sewing, painting, building, refinishing, recycling, recreating, budgeting, cooking, and eating healthful foods. And we would focus on leadership training for those of specific cultures who could more effectively reach and teach their own people.

The building process began during one of Minnesota's most severe winters. After rough-in carpenters completed their work, my innovative son continued with the insulating and the plumbing, and the rest of the family laid wood flooring and nailed up walls of paneling.

During two years of construction, we have felt God's presence and known the protection of His guardian angels, as family and friends have worked together.

We have made 1,500 tiles and the job has seemed endless! But most of the time we have been too busy to be discouraged.

We are still living in an unfinished house and frankly, I have been ashamed to invite people to come. But I have seen in the last six months that people do not care about the mess; they willingly put up with the inconvenience to share in our activities. Our Tall House is already being used by Life with Spice groups, peasant-painting classes, small retreat groups, and faithful friends from the city, as well as new friends from our rural church and community.

In one month alone we shared our home with over 120 different individuals. And there will be much more. I ache because part of me is still in north Minneapolis; yet I look with great anticipation to what God plans to do through our house in the woods. He continues to send broken lives to us, as if to remind us that wherever we are, if we ask Him, He will send hurting people into our hearts and homes.

The Tall House in the Woods *will* be finished. I can stop fretting. I have seen God use it in its unfinished condition. I am at peace.

Iris Fulcher and her husband spent their early years in England, but now live in Minnesota. They have three grown children. Iris serves as coordinator of Release Time Education in St. Paul, and ministers with the Women's Home League of the Salvation Army.

8

Two Hours Each Week— A Civil Right

"It was during the days of the blitz in England, with all its dangers, destruction, and uncertainty, that God began working in my life. I was a teenager, growing up in a thoroughly Christian home. Keeping the Lord's Day special, holy, and dedicated to God was an important part of our homelife.

"Toys were put away on Saturday, because early Sunday we all went to Sunday School, then stayed for church. We were taken to the afternoon Sunday School, the afternoon praise and testimony meeting, the evening street meeting, and then the evening service which crowned our day. Actually, we *lived* at the Salvation Army all day on Sundays, just walking home between services long enough to have a lunch.

"Can you understand how difficult it is for me to see shopping centers open, merchants plying their wares, and every sort of amusement establishment open and begging for business on the Lord's Day? I wonder if we are better off for having become so lax about the observance of His Day."

73

Bombs and Closed Churches

"I remember living in England 15 months after World War II started, when the bombing of London actually began. Every night, just as soon as it got dark, the sirens would go off. Then the bombs would come—maybe two or three at a time, but enough to make us aware that we could be attacked at any moment by a bomber. Many people spent hours in air-raid shelters. At times, maybe 100 planes would come over during the night. It was terrifying!"

Iris was full of fears as a young girl. The future looked bleak for her generation. Destruction was all around and the constant smoke of burning buildings filled the air with dread.

One Christmas Eve, last-minute shoppers packed a local Woolworth's store just a few blocks from their home. There was a direct hit on the store and over 200 people were killed! Iris says such experiences are never really forgotten.

The British government asked churches in the London area to close their doors, because they didn't want to have the people gathered together to become targets for the bombs.

"One Sunday at morning devotions, a daily occurrence in our family, my parents told us that the privilege of going to church had been taken away from us. A *privilege* to attend church? Yes, oh yes! It began to sink into my mind and heart that church attendance was indeed a blessing and a *privilege*.

"I went out for a walk and found my way to the beautiful door of the imposing Anglican church at the end of our block. Sure enough, I tried the door, but it was locked. It was as if God's Spirit was speaking to me—in fact, I believe it *was* God—and I responded in the quietness of my heart, 'Lord, if ever You should grant us the privilege of having a Sunday where I can open the door and go in and worship You, I will thank You so much. And I will serve You all my life. I know Lord, that it is only You that can keep me true, but I will do my best.'" Iris rejoiced when the churches were again allowed to hold services four weeks later.

Commitment to Christ

Iris didn't even have the hope of survival beyond the bombing raids. The bombs kept coming, day after day, devastating her world. En route to work one day, Iris passed a cemetery where a bomb had been dropped; she could see the unearthed bodies lying on the ground. It is still impossible for Iris to convey the feelings and fears of those who lived through the London Blitz. It was during those perilous days that her commitment to Christ was sealed.

Years later, the Fulcher family was led to America, and to St. Paul, Minnesota. They took their place in the Salvation Army Temple Corps there—Iris' husband Sidney in the band, and both Iris and Sidney in the Songsters.

The Call to Teach

Iris told me she received an invitation in 1957 to teach Release Time religious education classes. Iris says, "Until that time, I knew nothing about Release Time except that we had sent our children. When our eldest daughter Miriam came home from Release Time class each week, she seemed especially happy.

"I didn't feel really worthy of the assignment, and I had good reasons at home to reinforce my hesitation. My parents lived in our house, and my dad was not too well. Yet, it seemed that the Lord was directing me.

"When I arrived home from the first class I had taught, I was overcome with a sense of blessing and well-being. In the ensuing years, I have discovered that prompt obedience always brings blessing. God has provided all that I have needed. He has given me the time to study, and the desire to go the extra mile for Him each week."

In His plan and design, God called Iris into this work, which dovetailed exquisitely with her work in the Salvation Army.

When in 1977, the coordinator of Release Time Education in St. Paul became ill and was forced to leave her job, Iris was asked to assume this much greater challenge. She was already well-known for her years of effective work with the St. Paul Association of Evangelicals in a variety of capacities.

Expecting God to use her in this new way, Iris did become the Release Time Education coordinator for St. Paul. It has been challenging but sometimes discouraging work. Iris shares her needs regularly with a local prayer chain, requesting prayer that God would lead in selection of teachers, and that He would place them in the right schools. Last year there were three consultants who could not continue teaching or assisting for various reasons. It is becoming increasingly difficult to secure volunteers, and to find people who are committed to a humble task, who possess wisdom to move into a situation with tact and prudence, and who have a cooperative spirit.

The state law provides for two hours of religious instruction in school, with parents' consent, but many principals and teachers oppose this provision, feeling that such instruction should take place after school hours.

Iris feels strongly that the Release Time law is a good one—that the Word of God needs to be available to the unchurched child. In the 1978—1979 school year, 65 percent of the 753 children who attended Religious Release Time in the St. Paul schools were unchurched. This is a missionary work that cannot be abandoned.

Co-Workers and Encouragements

God has answered prayer and sent three capable and committed women to this work. One of them, Fran Moore, has taken the responsibility for two schools! Her influence has extended beyond the children's classes to teachers and parents. God has provided the use of a bus from the Union Gospel Mission. The driver, who has been a youth pastor, is teaching at the school. The bus now picks up a capacity cargo of 55 children, instead of the former 22. This is just one example of the blessing of God on this important work.

Iris wonders how much longer we will have the privilege of Release Time classes in our public schools, but her eyes light up when she tells about the children who are being taught and led to receive Christ right now through these classes. Recently, Iris visited a school to take part in the end of season celebration. After the refreshments were served, the principal of the school spoke to the children.

He said, "Children, your school is a wonderful place for you to learn. There we teach you reading, writing, mathematics, and many other things. But I am so grateful that your parents and your guardians realize that your education is not complete until you learn about God. I hope and pray that what you hear about in Release Time will take you to a church on Sundays, so that you can continue your education in learning about God."

Thank God for that principal and for others within our public schools who are committed to Jesus Christ, and who are encouraging Release Time Education as well as bearing witness to Christ in their daily contacts in school.

Iris tells of a St. Paul school Release Time bus driver who was having a discipline problem with the riders—the kids were creating chaos! The Release Time consultant began to speak to the children in her school about their behavior. She taught the children about heaven and hell, and the choice each child, individually, needed to make concerning Christ. She related the importance of following rules and respecting those in authority. She asked, "Do you want to follow the rules? You won't be able to do this by yourselves, but God sent us His Son, Jesus, to live and die for us. If you believe that He did this for you, and accept Him, and live for Him, He will help you."

The pastor of the church, Captain Marvin Dahl, was asked to explain the way of salvation. He asked if any children in the group wanted to accept Jesus right then. Out of the 60 children, 22 stood up and prayed with the leader! Many of us work for years and years, and are never able to say that we led 22 people to the Master.

Iris testifies, "I count it a privilege to serve the Lord as coordinator of this work. This is my third year, but I am ready to do it again if the Lord has this in mind for me. Imagine being given the opportunity to serve God in such delightful ways!"

Varied Ministries

Iris also continues working with the St. Paul Salvation Army Temple Corps by assuming responsibility for the Women's Home League. This service organization is dedicated to meeting family needs through worship, fellowship, and education. Recently, this group of women served more than 400 people (mostly senior citizens) a dinner free of charge! Morning prayer meetings and Bible study, and fun and field trips are included in Iris' busy schedule.

"How did the Lord get me ready for my life right now? I guess it began when I got my B.A. degree early in my teens. B.A. in my teens? Yes, God conferred upon me the privilege of being *born again* into His family—and I have been in the Saviour's schoolroom ever since!"

Iris is a builder. She steps out in faith to follow God's leading. She gives God all the glory for what has been accomplished through her life, knowing that it is not through her own abilities.

When Iris and I met to talk at a quiet conference center, she shared her burden of the challenge before us in public schools. "Daisy, we need more help in our Release Time ministry. So many women that we approach say, 'I work' and therefore they are not open to considering avenues of service. There have been times in my life when I have needed to work, also.

"But do you think there are God's women out there who might be willing to forego some 'things' to allow God to be their full-time Employer? Right now, I am happy that *this ministry is my work!*"

9
Release Time Religious Instruction

In Oakland, California public school students during the school day memorize Scripture, study Christ's pattern for prayer, and learn to apply biblical principles in everyday life. These children participate in weekly Religious Release Time classes.

Evangelicals in Oakland are utilizing an open door for religious education of public school students. The California Education Code allows pupils in the fourth, fifth, and sixth grades to be released from school upon the request of their parents for a religious instruction class one day per week. Children from 56 of Oakland's 60 public schools participate in Release Time Education.

Religious Release Time is not new. Release Time Education began in Gary, Indiana in 1913 and spread to other communities. The survival of Release Time has been a struggle. In various states, attempts have been made to ban the program, but the Supreme Court has upheld the opinion of lower courts that Release Time is constitutional.

Recently, there has developed an increased awareness that Release Time provides a means of keeping religious instruction in the public schools. Evelyn Carpenter, director of Oakland's Evangelical Release Time, receives many requests from across the country for information on how to begin classes. She suggests the following steps as a guide for program development:

1. Leadership. To successfully begin classes, there must be a dedicated individual or group with a concern for the religious education of children. "Directing Release Time Education involves long hours and many responsibilities," notes Mrs. Carpenter. "It's more than an eight-hour job."

2. Support. Anyone interested in starting Release Time should obtain endorsements from local churches. Churches provide much needed moral and financial support. The support of public officials and business and civic leaders is also beneficial. Broad-based community involvement will prove helpful in gaining approval of the program by school officials.

3. Facilities. In 1963 the Supreme Court ruled that while religious practices cannot be brought into the schools, schedules can be adjusted to allow students to receive religious education away from the school site. In order to conduct Release Time, facilities must be provided near the school. Classes are generally conducted in churches or homes located within walking distance of the school. Oakland has solved the problem of classroom space when there is no available church or home by using mobile classrooms. Two buses have been converted to classrooms.

4. Teachers. The success of an educational program depends upon its teachers. Release Time Education programs depend upon Christian men and women who generally volunteer their time as teachers. Teacher training is an integral part of Release Time instruction. Programs aim for a high standard of teacher performance since the children are leaving their public school classrooms for the most essential information they will ever learn.

Teacher recruitment is a vital step in program development. Churches are an excellent resource for securing teachers. The media can be used for teacher recruitment. Oakland has found that spot announcements on Christian radio stations, along with newspaper and billboard advertising, produce responses.

5. Curriculum. The purpose of Release Time is to provide children with the fourth "R," Religion; so selection of curriculum is important.

Since Release Time organizations function autonomously, each community selects its own material. Mrs. Carpenter recommends that those who are beginning a program consider using material developed especially for Release Time to avoid boring the children with repetition. Half of the children in Oakland's classes attend Sunday School or other religious activities. In Oakland boys and girls study *The Greatest Book in Pictures,* a three-year basic Bible course written exclusively for Release Time.

6. *Publicity.* Release Time can take place only if parents consent to their children being released. Materials must be prepared to inform parents. Communities that have been successful in starting programs have found that short, simple explanations are most effective. Evangelical Release Time of Oakland sends home a wallet-sized brochure which informs parents of what they need to know in seven sentences: what release time is, who sponsors it, who the teachers are, what is taught, and what the program's aims are. Later, children take home a simple parent permission form. Mrs. Carpenter states she has seen efforts to start Release Time fail because of complex explanations or consent forms.

7. *Presentation to School Officials.* School officials often know nothing about the concept of Release Time Education. Careful preparation for preliminary meetings with school personnel is essential. Information regarding state laws and court rulings on Release Time should be gathered. It is wise to have some knowledge about which school officials are likely to support or oppose the program, prior to the meeting. Strong opposition is common. Mrs. Carpenter recalls one occasion when 2,700 teachers signed a petition stating that Release Time interrupted the school schedule. Mrs. Carpenter dramatically countered this attack by indicating interruptions in the school day, caused by disrespectful, delinquent children. She argued that Release Time teaches children moral and spiritual values which foster courtesy, respect for authority, and good citizenship. After she finished her presentation, the school board voted unanimously in favor of Release Time Education.

Consideration of these steps has made it possible for Release Time to operate effectively in Oakland for 33 years. Mrs. Carpenter and others in California would like to see Release Time classes develop in every community across the nation. Mrs. Carpenter will provide further information to anyone who contacts Evangelical Release Time, 1925 Forty-First Avenue, Oakland, California 94601.

Betty Bottomly has been a military wife. When her husband retired from the armed services, Betty and her family settled on a California ranch, where they host retreats and conferences for military families.

10
They Follow a New Commander

"My Mom was a flag waver! And a chairman of her state chapter of the Daughters of the American Revolution. Why, she had the biggest troop of Girl Scouts in Manila, 65 American girls in the Philippines! Dad was an officer in the United States Army and Mom fought her own kind of battle!"

As Betty and I sat at her kitchen table drinking tea, Betty's face lit up recalling her mother and the indelible impressions made on her life. Betty grew up in the military lifestyle, with her father and brother—and now husband and son—all part of the armed forces. It was a transient, mobile life, but their Scottish heritage provided a fierce clannishness, with an "all for one and one for all" spirit of family that would stand Betty in good stead as the years of her own life unfolded.

MacArthur was commander in the Philippines, and there were days when Betty's dad golfed in a foursome destined to military greatness. A certain Colonel D.D. Eisenhower matched putting strokes on the green with her father.

World War II
Loyalty to country and respect for the flag were qualities of life that

Betty simply took for granted. When World War II was declared, it was natural for her to go right from the University of Kentucky to the Signal Corps in Washington. She became a cryptographer, with responsibility for helping to break codes. A promotion at age 23 put her in the astonishing responsibility of personnel counselor over 5,000 girls who had moved into the Washington area to work for the government. Betty became a confidante, employment agent, social director, housemother, and top sergeant.

During those years, Betty came to love a young field artillery soldier. After they were engaged to be married, she received word that he had been killed in France. Betty's world then fell apart; for the devastation of the war had invaded even the safety zone of her heart.

Was it an Ernest Hemingway fantasy, or the glamorous relief from the tyranny of the ordinary, that prompted a brokenhearted Betty to enter the service of the Red Cross? She doesn't know, but is quick to say that her time there was eventful, if not always glamorous!

Betty now feels that God was already preparing her for future leadership, when she was a Red Cross program director for servicemen's clubs overseas. Music, coffee, smiling faces—not exactly all the comforts of home—but they did the best they could for airmen and infantrymen coming back from mind-, body-, and soul-exhausting combat.

Romance Again

Heath Bottomly was traveling with his squadron via troopship to the Southwest Pacific. In his book *Prodigal Father,* he writes about his encounter with a Red Cross unit sharing the ship, and specifically, with one beautiful blond. Heath and Betty were both strong characters, and goal-oriented, and their romance was stormy. They both traveled in the war-torn Pacific and occasionally bumped into one another, each time getting better acquainted.

Betty married her Bo (a name she conferred on Heath at first meeting because she couldn't remember his last name) in a little bombed-out church in Manila.

Five children were born to Betty and Heath. Typically a military man, Dad fought on the other side of the world during the frightening days of the Vietnam struggle. Mother managed a single-parent home, and threw her energies into Girl Scouting. Lessons learned in her "program directing days" helped considerably when putting together camp-outs for 400 girls!

1965

Roc Bottomly became a cadet at the Air Force Academy. Betty had let her eldest son go, confident that his desire to pursue a career in the United States Air Force was a wise plan. Roc's roommate was a Christian who was involved in Bible study with the Christian organization, "Navigators." In the midst of floor scrubbing duty, his roommate told Roc that Jesus Christ had died for him, and challenged Roc to accept Christ as Saviour.

Roc's young life was turned around as he became the first born again member of the Bottomly family. Only three months later, he was instrumental in winning his brother and two sisters to the Lord.

Meanwhile, Colonel Bottomly was in the thick of the action in Vietnam. A West Pointer, and commander of the most aggressive and effective fighter wing in Vietnam, he had disregarded orders about flying into enemy territory! A reprimand and a threatened court-martial devastated super achiever Bo.

How did he have the courage in the midst of humiliation to pick up the telephone and call across the Pacific, to ask for help from his son? The mighty sovereign God was at work, and Colonel Bottomly was gently but decisively led to Jesus Christ.

Within a few days, Bo's boss flew to the base to reconsider the reprimand. In that instant new orders were received which read that because of the enemy's violations of the no-firing agreement, American airmen were authorized to retaliate. So Bo was saved from court-martial and his career was again secure. What a miracle! God was sealing Bo's commitment!

Meanwhile, although Betty and Bo's marriage had been weakened by prolonged separation, Betty was determined to "stick with it" and give their five children a united home. Bo had not revealed his commitment to Christ, but Betty did know from his letters that there had been a change in him that she could not define.

New Life for Betty

Bo's transfer to Norton Air Force Base in Southern California necessitated a cross-country trip and another house-hunting expedition. Providentially, the *perfect* house was found in the shadow of Arrowhead Springs (the Campus Crusade for Christ headquarters) nestled in the San Bernardino mountains.

Their daughter passed the word along to Dorothy Mayelle that Betty was new in the area. Dorothy and her husband were on Campus

Crusade staff to work with military personnel, and to present Christ
to those in the armed forces. It did not take long for Betty to realize
her need for a Saviour and to accept Jesus Christ as the Lord of her
heart and life. Betty was nurtured as a baby Christian by Vonette
Bright, Dorothy, and others of the Crusade staff. They patiently
discipled and led Betty from a position of strong self-sufficiency to a
deep and definite walk with the Lord.

Soon the Bottomly home became a haven for high school young
people that daughters Kris and Sheri and son Kirk brought home
from the student life ministry on their campuses.

Bo's ministry broadened and he was encouraged to cooperate in
making a movie of his life. He began traveling and speaking widely,
using the movie and his subsequent book to minister to many people
faced with difficult life situations.

God was blessing their lives, but they began to dream about an
enlarged ministry after Bo's retirement. In the armed forces, retirement often means the beginning of a second or third career. Since
they loved horses, a small *ranch* with horses seemed to be the ideal
jumping-off spot for all sorts of ministries.

The real estate agent called with a lead in Arizona—just the place!
Then another possibility in Colorado, and Bo and Betty were off to
explore. But when they drove up a narrow, winding mountain road in
a cranny of Boulder Creek, California, they knew they wanted to live
in the Redwoods.

Redwood Ranch

Betty's experiences had led her to be concerned for the young people
who were a part of the military community in our country. Betty was
burdened for the many military wives whose transient lifestyles and
uncertain surroundings brought pressures on home and family that
often seemed impossible to withstand. She longed to share Christ
more and more effectively. She was deeply interested in rebuilding
the moral walls of protection in our society that had been affected by
the "situation ethics" philosophy of life. The ranch in Boulder Creek
was indeed the answer.

But before they moved to Spring Hill Ranch, Bev, a fledgling
Campus Crusade staffer, was sent to Norton Air Force Base to work
with the service people on the base. Viki Bottomly learned of Bev's
need for housing and suggested that she move into the sixth bedroom
of their home in San Bernardino. Bev fell in love with the entire

family. But she was especially taken with Roc—who wasn't even living at home!

After a time, Bev was very upset to find that she was being transferred north from Norton to Presidio of Monterey in Monterey, California. That meant leaving the family and home she had come to claim as her own. But then she heard the thrilling news—Betty and Bo had actually purchased the ranch in the Santa Cruz Mountains, just 50 miles from the Presidio of Monterey!

Betty figured that the ranch could be adapted to accommodate at least 50 people for retreats and miniconferences. They didn't need to wonder where "retreatees" would come from. God had a plan all worked out.

At the Monterey Presidio, the United States operates the largest defense language institute in the country. The armed forces' cream of the crop is assigned there for as long as 18 months. Arabic, Russian, Mandarin, Korean, Japanese and a variety of other languages are taught in highly accelerated courses.

When Bev called to ask if she could bring a group of these young women to the ranch for a weekend retreat, Betty was delighted, and their dream of ministering to the military began to be fulfilled.

Bev has become Roc's wife, and presently Roc is attending Dallas Seminary in preparation for his ministry. They have become parents of three children, and return often to encourage and be refreshed at Spring Hill Ranch in Boulder Creek.

Betty sees God's hand shaping and building individual lives. In 1979, over 1,200 people spent some time in retreats and conferences at their home. All the years of military mobility provided the necessary training for this demanding life of total availability to the Lord. Church staffs, college students, and service people find their way to the comfortable yellow and white house on the hill. An average of two retreats a month keeps Betty dusting and vacuuming, but equal time is given to teaching Sunday School, leading Bible study discussions, and keeping in touch with their grown children.

"Have Another Cup, Daisy?"

As Betty and I sat enjoying our second cup of tea, I looked around at her kitchen. The cupboard doors were on the floor. The gaping hole that would soon accommodate a more adequate oven tried to smile.

"Betty, your kitchen is a sight!"

"Wait until you see it in about two weeks, Daisy."

"But you said you were having 15 people for a retreat this weekend!"

"Don't you think it was incredible of God to send a group that has planned a weekend fast?"

What a lady!

Malettor Cross and her husband, with several of their children, are ministering at the Detroit Afro-American Mission, which they founded.

11

Black America Is Still Suffering

"In our one room church in Tennessee, four classes met in four corners, but the 'old folks' always got the choir loft. In that clapboard sanctuary I received the only Sunday School training I can remember."

- "Okay, Brother, hear it again! 'God who at sundry times in divers manners, spake in time past . . .'"
- "Just a minute, Brother, you have talked too much. Let's hear from the preacher now!"
- "Well, friends, let us consider this passage from another angle."
- "GOD, WHO AT SUNDRY TIMES AND IN DIVERS MANNERS SPAKE IN TIME PAST UNTO THE FATHERS BY THE PROPHETS, hath in these last days spoken unto us by His Son. . . ." (Heb. 1:1, KJV).

"This was about as 'divers' a manner as God had ever spoken in, and I sat on the edge of my seat to listen to the outcome of the argument. Really it wasn't an argument, but a four-cornered pooling of ignorance. The winner was the loudest shouter.

"The only verse I can remember learning as a child is Hebrews 1:1. God has been dealing with me in 'divers' manners ever since I accepted Jesus as my Saviour when I was 11 years old."

Memories

Malettor Cross sat curled up on the bed near me as we visited and shared in each other's lives in her home state of Michigan. I was picking her brain to see what made her tick, this mother of 11 children, working full time in the Detroit Afro-American Mission with her husband, Haman. Malettor is a builder, of families and of the kingdom of God; she is working "on the wall" near her own home.

Speaking out of her rich memory bank, she told how her granddaddy, the son of a slave, had been a sharecropper in Georgia. The Ku Klux Klan had terrorized her father's home neighborhood, and even at 87 he could recall hearing about floggings.

"I had never heard the Scripture about being careful not to marry an unbeliever—or about being unequally yoked. But after Haman and I were married, I knew something was wrong in our home. As I said, Jesus had come to be my Saviour when I was just a little girl, but I had had no training, and certainly no joy in the Lord. The Holy Spirit kept nudging me, and I guess I felt that if Haman could accept Christ, we could begin to live for the Lord. My mother would have been concerned about our marriage I know, but Haman was such a goody-goody, she didn't even think to ask him if he was a Christian!"

Malettor felt inadequate to lead anyone to the Lord, much less her own husband! They loved each other a great deal, so Haman was willing to please Malettor by going regularly to a little church with her. On the side, she let the preacher in on her concern for Haman's salvation.

After church one morning, the old preacher invited Haman into his little corner study in the rear of the church. "Sit down, Haman, I want to ask you some questions!" Haman hesitated with hat in hand, but pulled up a chair.

"Brother, are you drinking?" asked the preacher.

"Nope, I gave that up, except for a beer or two on the weekend, maybe."

"Young man, do you chase women?"

"No sir, I stopped doing that when I was in the navy."

"Young man, how about gambling—are you wasting your money gambling?"

"No, no, I'm just working hard and supporting my family!" The questions and answers flew back and forth, and with every challenge, Haman became more unnerved.

Finally, his flashing black eyes focusing on the young man's, the old preacher charged, "Brother, you are going to hell for NOTHING."

The preacher then led Haman down the "Roman Road" to his salvation. That day the preacher had shown him that he had the "zeal of God" but it was not according to knowledge (see Rom. 10:2, KJV).

A Young Family

In a spirit of adventure, newlyweds Malettor and Haman left Tennessee and looked to the West Coast. Sidetracked by the opportunity to earn some money to help with the trip, Haman went to work in the Ford plant in Detroit. They never left Michigan, as Detroit became home to Haman, Malettor, and by now, their first child.

As a result of their Christian faith, their family life did change, but they had no discipling or consistent teaching in the Word. The Holy Spirit began to disturb Malettor and one day she met Haman as he came home from work. "Haman, I want to live a good life, a different life, a clean life."

Now, Malettor was desiring to live for Jesus, but she did not plan to get fanatical about it! And she was not prepared for Haman's response. It seemed as if her world began to turn upside down. Haman began to assume the spiritual leadership of their family. Malettor still wanted a toehold in the world. This turnabout led to Malettor's disillusionment with the established church. It was intruding into their home and she was not so sure that the corruption and hypocrisy in the church was any less than she saw in the world.

"We had several children by then, and I decided that I would just try to teach them at home. No, Daisy, I never felt that I would go out and work to give them more materially. God has always put it in my heart to be a homemaker. Haman was a laborer at the Ford Company, and we were raising six children. Usually, Haman was laid off for three months during the winter, but we have never had to go outside for help in making ends meet.

"Sometimes, I am asked, 'Malettor, how can you live hand-to-mouth, like this? How have you made it all these years, living that way?' I just reply, 'As long as it's God's hand and my mouth, why should I care?' "

This tall, distinguished, middle-aged grandmother began to fix her hair, but she kept talking. "Daisy, you have never seen a sparrow with a lunch pail under his arm, have you?

"In 1956, God put a desire in my heart to reach children, and by His plan, Haman found a Child Evangelism magazine on a rack. He bought it, and I read it cover to cover, even the advertisements, and started a Bible club right away.

God's Barn
In 1964, "God's Barn" was "laid in their laps." In a donated building in downtown Detroit, Haman and Malettor began to teach Bible classes. "All we had for resources were Jesus and babies! And the Holy Spirit for our Teacher."

Even with all her household responsibilities, Malettor started sewing classes for the neighborhood women. Almost everyone knew how hard it was for the Crosses to clothe their growing family, so people gave them bags and bags of good clothes. Malettor and others would sort the clothes. Then after a Gospel service, they would open the "Barn Door," to allow the congregation to choose some of the clothing free of charge.

"Malettor, where did these ladies come from to get these clothes?"

"God gave us the idea, Daisy. We put little ads in the paper, and in the school newsletter, saying that if there were people whose kids couldn't go to school because they had no clothes, they could come and hear the Word of God, and then get the clothes. We believe that 'faith cometh by hearing, and hearing by the Word of God' (Rom. 10:17, KJV). What the people did with the Word was their responsibility, but we had to give it out. It isn't fair to just give people things when what they need most is the Gospel."

Need for Teachers
As we talked about the motivation for their presently growing work, Malettor pondered and then the light gleamed in her eyes: she quoted, "Where there is no vision, the people perish" (Prov. 29:18, KJV).

Malettor continued to think out loud: "The need is overwhelming for gut-level Bible teaching. The Word of God has not been taught to the blacks enough to bring about changed lives. The black community has been exploited by its own people and others. That is not to say that God has not raised up some fine, well-educated black teachers and preachers. But there have been so many others who have taught the Word when it has benefited *them,* for their *own* support, and not the benefit of the hearer."

Mrs. Cross was now into her element. This was the passion of her heart—*to teach teachers!* She was talking so fast and vibrantly, I had a hard time keeping up with her. . . .

"Yes, Daisy, that is what it is all about! In our conferences where we are trying to get black women to teach other black women, we want to 'scratch where it itches!' We want to teach women not only how to *be* Christians, but *how to live as Christians.* . . . 'As ye have therefore received Christ Jesus the Lord, so walk ye in Him' (Col. 2:6, KJV). They ask, 'How, Mrs. Cross, how are we to walk?' and I tell them, 'Step by step with the Word; not by opinions or fads, but with the Word!'

"That is my excitement now. I have two classes, one to train children's teachers, and one to train Bible class instructors. I have let all my ladies know that they are expected to go out and teach others. I tell them to activate 2 Timothy 2:2—to go and teach others."

Response to Need

How did God call the Cross family into this ministry? The answer was simple. "We were doing what God had wanted us to do, and He just led us one step farther." A certain church in Detroit offered to take on Haman's support. He did the janitor work for the church, and took his earnings home to Malettor and their 10 children. Then he did the work in downtown Detroit full time!

The Detroit Afro-American Mission was born in that donated downtown Detroit house, right in the middle of the ghetto. Riots in the 60s tore the city to pieces. The walls of human dignity and morality were broken down. Malettor spoke with emotion, charged with deep conviction:

"I know my people, and I know the needs of my people. I know how they need to *know* the Lord, not guess, not hope, not hang on, but relax in the Lord. I am not an educated person, but I tell you, with stammering lips, with buckling knees, if God gives the grace, the power and the wisdom, I am going everywhere He sends me to rescue my people.

"Daisy, there's a verse in Nehemiah that says it for me: 'Send some to those who have nothing prepared' (Neh. 8:10, NIV). And I am going to do just that.

"I am sick and tired of seeing the emphasis being put everywhere but where it should be. The years of the riots, as damning as they were, woke America up. But now, we have been rocked back to sleep and black America is still suffering."

Sufferings of Black America

Intrigued, but half afraid of how she might answer my next question, I led her to amplify her statement. "Tell me ways in which you feel black America is suffering right now, with all the government aid, and with the loud voices of effective black leaders being heard in our land."

"Daisy, black America is suffering because we have been given tools that we don't know how to use. The tool most misused is education. I am 140 percent in favor of education, but education without Christ is dangerous! I do not hold the government responsible for this. Secular education is doing its job, but Christian education for blacks is sorely lacking. Our homes are failing because we are sending our young people off to adulthood without having educated them in the Word of God."

When I asked Malettor about the other tools that had been handed to blacks, she was quick to reply that the welfare system was destroying a man's pride in his work, because a man wants to work to feel like a man. She strongly advocates that jobs be provided, in place of handouts, to relieve the suffering poor and hungry. Unemployment among blacks *is* higher than in other groups. The phrase, "Blacks are the last ones hired, the first ones fired," reflects truth.

What Can a Mission Do?

What is the Detroit Afro-American Mission seeking to do about the problems of the black people in their community? Malettor and Haman's work is a total-person, total-family outreach ministry. The mission was incorporated in 1964, and in 1968 Haman was "set free" from other work, to devote full time to this ministry.

Those people who come to the mission on Tuesdays and Thursdays of each week are being trained how to use the Word of God. They are taught that there is no need to learn to defend the Word; the Word defends itself. The Christian is to *use* the Scripture. The mission works to equip the saints.

Since the riots in the 60s, black hatred toward whites has stirred up and fed resentment. It is nearly impossible now for a white person to run across the tracks and say, "What you people need is Jesus," and then run back. So the best idea is to teach the blacks to teach others. Malettor has never believed that only blacks can minister to blacks. But because of increasing racial hostility, it seems sensible to train those already living in an area to reach others.

"I feel like Paul who said that he was willing to give up everything he had for the sake of his people. That is what we want to do. We want to share everything we have, without asking for government help or input. We can see that to take even a little government money means that the government would exert some authority over our work, and little by little, they would gain more jurisdiction over what we are doing. It is God's work, and it is growing."

While the Crosses distribute clothing, furniture, and food, they emphasize that theirs is primarily a building and training ministry. Two methods that they often use are:

Block parties—they move in with portable sports equipment. (Portable basketball hoops, portable volleyball nets—you name it!) They set up a playground on one city block, with the cooperation of the police department. They take along a staff of trained workers and gather in hundreds of young people that way.

Backyard clubs—they have as many as eight in a summer, five days each, led by a trained threesome from the mission.

Malettor and Haman Cross have been delighted to enlist their oldest son as administrator of the mission. At least 30 people are volunteer teachers and workers.

The mission has already been able to send a team of trained staff to begin two other churches in the Detroit area.

The Cross family has been a laboratory experience in this "construction" process. All 11 children know the Lord. Haman and Malettor have made rules in their home, and have expected their children to follow them. One of their children is a college graduate, four are in college now, and one son is in pre-med. Their son-in-law is the Boys' Brigade leader in the mission, while their daughter leads Pioneer Girls.

As Malettor lovingly and glowingly gave me a rundown on their family and their various works for the Lord, I thanked God for this woman. Of Malettor it can truly be said:

> Strength and honor are her clothing. . . . Her children arise up, and call her blessed; her husband also, and he praiseth her (Prov. 31:25, 28, KJV).

Eleanor Sams is married and has four children. She is a college teacher by profession, in the field of sociology and social work, as well as a researcher and lecturer. Residing in San Francisco, she is the editor of Current, *a newsletter for the Christian community.*

12
Influence Is What It's All About

She walks tall and with authority. I met Eleanor Sams in the summer of 1979, in San Francisco, where she makes her home with her husband and their four children.

Sociology and social work have been her fields, but teaching at a San Francisco College has occupied much of her time in recent years.

Eleanor is a communicator, and is able and articulate. She has a commitment to her Lord, her family, her country, and to her black brothers and sisters.

You may feel that public life, public speaking, and persuasive writing are not for you. Read Eleanor's story and consider *your* potential influence, in simple but specific ways. *Influence* is what it is all about, after all!

Eleanor's Story
My motivation comes from my roots. My mother and grandmother were both Christian women who were civically and politically involved.

My grandmother was a founding member of the Women's Political

Study Club. This organization was formed by a group of black women in Los Angeles to study political issues and then take action.

I can remember as a child sitting in my grandmother's living room on numerous occasions, listening to a political candidate present his platform. I will never forget the excitement of the night that James Roosevelt, son of Franklin Delano Roosevelt, spoke to a group of people at Grandmother's home. As he arrived I exclaimed, *"President Roosevelt's son is really here!"*

The occasion had a strong effect on me, because I began to realize that what ordinary people thought and felt was extremely important to political figures. This political precociousness has sometimes proved to be an embarrassment. People look at me rather strangely when I begin to describe, in vivid detail, an election that took place when I was five years old. I explain that I grew up in a very politically conscious family.

Mealtimes were often the occasion for debate on current issues. It was this discussion time that prepared me to be an orator and debater in high school. My sense of social responsibility matured during my years at U.C.L.A. and through my association with Adeline Gunther, executive secretary of the University Religious Conference. I was active in two interfaith projects of the university, which were designed to promote brotherhood between the United States and India.

"Gram," as Adeline was affectionately referred to by several generations of students, challenged me to speak out on moral and social issues. Gram believed that if she could spend her time with students who had leadership qualities, she could ultimately influence the community and society. I will not forget sitting in her home at the end of my senior year in college, hearing her say to a small group of us, "You are here because one day you will have responsible positions. Someday you will have occasion to make a decision which will have far-reaching moral and social implications, if you have the courage to stand by your convictions."

I sat in that room, glanced around the circle, and thought about the others: *He will be a judge, she will be married to a rich business tycoon, but I cannot see myself in a responsible position, affecting the community or large numbers of people. There is no way that could ever happen to me.*

A Memo
Twelve years later, I was to recall Gram's statement! As a consultant

for the State Department of Social Welfare, I was startled to see the use of a racially derogatory term on a form. The use of this term had official approval. I looked at the form and recalled several typists who had said to me, "Every time I have to type that word, I feel so degraded and so terrible—but there is nothing I can do!"

Were they, in fact, powerless? Could they not do a thing to change official state policy? I realized that I had the power to express my negative reactions to the use of the term, and that somebody would respond to a memo that I wrote. As I contemplated writing a memo, I began to think, *Oh, that's a stupid thing to do. So you write a memo—what difference does it make? Don't rock the boat; you are a probationary employee. What's the point? You'll be called a militant, a troublemaker.*

These thoughts and others raced through my head. It had been my style to act on issues in a quiet, unobtrusive fashion. I have never been afraid to speak up for my convictions, but I knew this was a very volatile and emotionally charged area. The more I sat there, the more I could here Gram's voice. . . . This was my moment of truth! I *could* do something. I could stand up for my convictions.

So I wrote the memo, and since this was a government bureaucracy, the memo had to "go through channels." The first person to see it was my immediate supervisor who was a very stern, unsmiling, black woman. She suggested that I reconsider sending it. For a moment I wavered. *Why risk embarrassment? Is it worth it? Why risk a reprimand from the area director?* Then I thought, *No, someone has to express in writing that these forms are insulting to minority employees. Let it go through.*

A few days later the director called me to his office. I was apprehensive, I'll admit. After I sat down, he looked at me, then began, "I'd like to tell you that I am really delighted that you wrote this memo—and I want to send a supporting letter requesting that this term be deleted from forms in the future." He said that he would also send a cover letter to all the area directors in the department, in the State of California.

When the state director received our memo, he sent a personal note to me saying that he approved of my position, and was directing a letter to the bureau that prepared the forms.

Months later, having forgotten all about the memo, I was preparing to leave the agency to go to another job. Another personal letter came, this time from the director of the Bureau of Criminal

Identification, stating that I was the first person in the history of the state to ever complain about the term. His letter indicated that the policy of the department had been changed, and that the terminology I objected to would no longer be used. That incident has given me the courage on numerous occasions since then to speak out for my convictions.

As mother of four, I am concerned about humanistic trends in education. As a citizen, I care about what is being decided for Americans in the halls of legislatures, and in the United States Congress. As a Christian, I care when the rights of God's people seem to be threatened.

I am concerned about the court decisions, the legislation, and the actions of individuals and organizations which are shifting control from the family, the church, and the community to the state and the federal government. I am concerned that the Christian community seems to be uniformed about what is actually taking place.

There are several reasons for this. One of the most obvious is the rapid pace at which change takes place, making it impossible to keep totally abreast of vital issues and events. Today's headline is tomorrow's history.

Next, there has been a shift in the source of decision-making and power. By this I mean that in the past many of the vital decisions regarding education were made by local school boards within a community. This is no longer true. Increasingly, decisions regarding public schools are being made at the state or federal level. Local school boards function primarily to carry out the state and federal legislation and directives.

The same is true in the spheres of health and welfare. Responsibility has shifted from the community, and even the state has lessening power and control over health and welfare services. Local citizens are not actively involved in many areas of the decision-making process in our society today.

Popular Voter Initiative

This shift in power toward state and federal levels has caused frustration among many groups, so there has been a growing trend toward legislation through the ballot. We are increasingly seeing voters attempting to make their wishes and desires become law through the initiative process. While there is much to be said in favor of the initiative process, it does mean that there is a shift of power from the legislature to the ballot. With this shift in power, from our elected legislators to the voter, comes dramatic change in the way individuals and pressure groups can make concerns known.

When laws are being made through the normal legislative process, special interest groups will contact elected representatives to voice their concerns. However, when laws are being made through the ballot initiative process, special interests and concerns have to be made known either through the media or through various grass roots networks of communication and through public gatherings to inform the voters.

I decided to focus upon developing a communication network for Christians, to inform them about issues and events which concern the Christian community. The vehicle for doing this is a newsletter titled *Current*. I chose this title because the dictionary defines the word as, "a passing from hand to hand or from mouth to mouth among the public." My intent is that people will read the newsletter and will share its content with others.

Recently, through *Current* I was able to alert Christians to an initiative that would seriously affect religious education in California. I first became aware of this initiative when I attended a meeting at my son's parochial school. Attendance at the meeting was compulsory. Parents were told to attend or their children would not receive report cards. I was surprised when I saw that the purpose of the meeting was to inform the families about an initiative which was designed to do a number of things:

- It would give parents control of their children's curriculums.
- It would be the means for saving the public schools (parents would be given vouchers so that they could send their children to the school of their choice).
- It would eliminate the use of property tax support to public schools.

As I listened to the supporters of this move, I realized that they were using particular religious schools as a means on the petition to qualify the initiative for the ballot. As I looked around the room, I could see from watching people's faces that they did not understand much of what was said about this initiative. The speaker quickly mentioned that if a school accepted a voucher it could no longer require students to profess a belief or participate in symbolic religious ceremonies. I was surprised that the religious school which my son was attending would support the initiative. When I asked for a clarification, the speaker eluded my question, suggesting that parents sign the petition and then let the courts settle the constitutional question of whether religious schools could receive vouchers.

The speaker presenting the initiative was an attorney who had been well versed on the subject. Because he was so courteous, it was very difficult to challenge the pro-initiative position. It soon became evident that a well-organized and well-financed group of people was backing this measure.

However, they were relying primarily upon the signatures of the religious community to qualify the initiative for the ballot. The initiative was worded in such a way that the average person would not understand the underlying issue. I decided to take a stand against the measure because it represented a clear threat to religious education. But I was also concerned because of the direct attempt to manipulate the religious community into supporting a measure that was not in its best interest. I saw a definite attempt to deceive and distort, in both the summary and the title of the initiative. (It should be noted that the summary and the title are known as the only two things that most people consider when they vote on an initiative.)

Tools for Action

I had to ask myself, *How does one woman lead a campaign against a well-organized effort?* My conclusion was that I had effective tools at my disposal. First, I had available the right *communication* with my heavenly Father through prayer. The first line of attack was to begin intercessory prayer regarding this matter. I asked other Christians to join me in prayer that this initiative would not be passed.

Secondly, I could use the *pen*. I began to realize that effective stands against injustice and wrongs, and stands for rights have been taken by individuals picking up their pens—not by writing a book or volume, but by writing articles, handbills and letters. I decided that my work toward right and justice would be done with the pen. I would alert Christians to the dangers threatening their freedom.

I had *contacts*—pastors, Bible study teachers, and other key lay people, whom I could alert about the issues. I asked them to tell everyone they contacted about the initiative, so that by word of mouth and these handbills, the message could spread. I suggested that they telephone others, some within their family and neighborhood, and one or two in other parts of the state. Personal communication is vitally important, both to inform and to persuade.

A fourth tool is *research*. I have developed a workshop to help others perfect skills for efficiency and credibility. Most people can write an effective article or newsletter by following these three basic principles:

1. Be alert. 2. Be accurate. 3. Be attractive.

Not enough can be said about the need for careful research on current issues. Be accurate, and you will achieve credibility. When writing letters or handbills, be careful with grammar and set up your presentation attractively. The credibility of the author is determined by how objectively the facts are presented and how accurate the data is.

Be sure names are spelled correctly, and that dates, places, and times are correct. Give attention to each detail. Get acquainted with your public library and its research possibilities.

Since we are bombarded with more information than we can possibly process, it is extremely important that we zero in on certain key areas of information, and then organize the material. Read, read, read newspapers and magazine articles. Watch television news. Make a file of what you are reading and learning. Develop a clipping file. Clip while you read, and avoid clutter by filing according to subject in folders. Become informed as thoroughly as possible on at least one single area of concern. Then continue in prayer, and begin to use your pen to influence for good.

Nehemiah and the people rebuilding the wall of Jerusalem were slowed in their efforts because they had to stop and use their swords in defense against their enemies (see Neh. 4:13-18). We have a weapon in our battle against injustice that is mightier than the sword—the pen of the informed citizen.

Building Blocks You Can Place

The Underprivileged/The Inner City
1. Consider opening your home as a ministry. Reach out to your neighbors. Imagine a new, untried use of some of your artistic gifts.
2. Attend some services in a multiracial church.
3. Walk through the inner-city area near you. Discover what ministry opportunities are available and how God could use you. Perhaps you should consider moving to the inner city.
4. Become acquainted with Bible study resource materials, such as Life with Spice.
5. Support a local rescue mission in your area—prayerfully, financially, and with your volunteer services.
6. Additional resources:
   National Association of Christians in Social Work, P.O. Box 84, Wheaton, Illinois 60187.
   Life with Spice, Scripture Press Publications, 1825 College Avenue, Wheaton, Illinois 60187.

Religious Release Time Classes
1. Learn to teach others!
2. Investigate to see what your state allows for religious education of children in public schools.
3. Offer to lead a children's class, using materials such as Child Evangelism Fellowship provides.
4. Consider rearranging your priorities to allow time to be involved in a ministry for the Lord. Perhaps this will involve not taking on employment, or cutting back your job hours.

5. Additional resources:
Evangelical Release Time (Mrs. Evelyn Carpenter, Director), 1925 Forty-First Ave., Oakland, California 94601.
Child Evangelism Fellowship, P.O. Box 348, Warrenton, Missouri 63383.
Evangelical Released-Time Education (Long Beach Chapter), P.O. Box 5106, Long Beach, California 90805.

Co-Workers/Military People
1. Practice the gift of hospitality.
2. Sharpen your witnessing skills. Ask the Lord to give you courage to share your faith, and then do it!
3. Endeavor to minister to military personnel—either in person or by a letter or surprise "care package."
4. Additional resources:
NAE Commission on Chaplaincy (Chaplain Ervin Ingebretson), 1430 K St., N.W., Washington, D.C. 20005.
Overseas Christian Servicemen's Centers, Inc., P.O. Box 19188, Denver, Colorado 80219.
Christian Serviceman's Fellowship, 5211 W. St. Joseph, Lansing, Michigan 48917.
Christian Military Fellowship, P.O. Box 36440, Denver, Colorado 80236.

Community Outreach
1. Follow Eleanor Sams' suggestions for researching and writing. Try composing a concise flyer on an issue about which you are concerned.
2. Read, clip, and begin a filing system to keep your information usable.
3. Participate in your local PTA and other community organizations. Be informed and be a Christian influence.

SECTION III

WHO HAS RIGHTS?

JULIE TURNQUIST, a surgical nurse facing the issue of abortion on demand, articulates the rights of the unborn child and the assisting nurse.

LOUISE MATSON, as an immigrant from a Communistic country, expresses the rights of a person to have religious freedom.

GLADYS DICKELMAN is concerned for the rights of women and their families.

BEV LAHAYE focuses on rights of young people and children in today's changing society.

NORMA GABLER and her husband have devoted many years to the rights of the schoolchild to receive accurate information in the learning process.

Nehemiah said, "They all thought they could frighten us so that our hands would cease from pursuing the work. Therefore, may God strengthen my hands." Nehemiah 6:9, BERK

Julie Turnquist is a Minneapolis-based nurse, who has held a variety of hospital nursing positions during the last 25 years. She is also on the staff of Navigators, a Christian organization involved in training young adults.

13

Human Life
in Pieces

In 1973, Julie Turnquist was head surgical nurse at a private hospital in Minneapolis. During Julie's 18 years as a nurse, she had on rare occasion assisted in abortions which were considered necessary for health reasons by the medical review board of the hospital. Such abortions were regarded as surgeries and were subjected to the same standards of review as other operations.

After the Supreme Court decision in 1973 which struck down restrictive state laws on abortion, Julie saw that more very young women were coming asking for abortions. Their reasons differed greatly from the reasons permitted under the medical review board. They wanted abortions on demand. Their cases were not reviewed by the doctors. It was a matter of putting down their money for services rendered.

Although the number of requests for abortions had increased, the hospital staff had not performed very many before Julie began to seek guidance from the Lord about this question. She searched the Scriptures for answers and found three sections that became convincing proof to her of the wrongness of abortion on demand.

The Lord said to Jeremiah, "Before I fashioned you in the womb I knew you, and before you were born I dedicated you; I designated you for a prophet to the nations" (Jer. 1:5, BERK).

In Psalm 139, David wrote of God seeing him before he was born: "Thou didst possess my inward parts and didst weave me in my mother's womb. I praise Thee because I have been fearfully and wonderfully made. . . . My bones were not hidden from Thee when I was made in secrecy and intricately fashioned in utter seclusion" (vv. 13-15, BERK).

The third portion of Scripture was in Luke 1. The angel announced to the Virgin Mary that she would conceive a child who would be the Holy One of Israel, the Son of the Highest, the One who would receive the throne of His father David.

The intimate knowledge God expressed of these children yet unborn, was what Julie needed to persuade her that she had to do something to protest the rising number of abortions in her hospital. She also became convinced that a devoted Christian would not pursue or perform abortion on demand.

One other factor that added to her conviction was the feeling that came over her when she would go down to the pathology lab after an abortion, and see the bits of arms, legs, eyes, and fingers in a small jar. She felt as if she was in a butcher shop, seeing human life in small pieces. And she knew that such butchery was not God's work.

Within months after the Supreme Court decision, Julie made a list of the nurses in surgery and asked permission of her supervisor to poll these 12 nurses, on their readiness to assist in abortions. Of the 12, 10 said they would not assist. The resistance of the nurses curtailed sharply the number of abortions which could be done.

Julie's courageous act was noted by the news media, broadcast over radio stations, and printed in magazines and church papers. She had a large mail response from various parts of the world.

Looking back on this now, Julie expresses her own gratefulness that someone cared about life when she was born—as a very premature baby. She believes that life is eternal, and that God is the only One who determines the span of life. Man has no right to terminate a life, for God has His purposes for people, even into old age.

Abortion: The Blight of America
In March 1980, Victor Books released *Life in the Balance* by James Hefley. I quote from chapter 3.

Get ready for a global shock! Over 40 million babies were deliberately aborted in 1978, one in every four pregnancies. In the United States alone, a million were put to death, most of them for the convenience of the mother. This brings to 6 million the number of fetuses deliberately aborted in the U.S. since the Supreme Court struck down restrictive state laws on abortion in 1973. Harold O. J. Brown, chairman of the Christian Action Council, ominously comments: "America has now destroyed more innocent lives through abortion than Hitler did in his extermination chambers" (open letter, February 20, 1979).

Commercial abortion mills advertising pregnancy testing and "counseling" thrive in cities with populations over 100,000. Scores of self-advertised clinics and counseling centers operate in large metropolises such as New York City, where abortions out-numbered births in 1975. They are supposed to be strictly regulated; in actual fact, many are little better than the back-alley butchers who operated before abortion became legal.

Means of Abortion

Abortion is no new practice. Archeologists have uncovered evidence that mercury was used as an abortifacient as early as 3,000 B.C. An Assyrian manuscript from 1,500 B.C. recommends insertion of acacia tips which form lactic acid when dissolved in water. Some contraceptive jellies contain lactic acid.

Modern methods are far more successful and much safer for the pregnant woman. The intrauterine (IUD) loops and "morning after" pills expel the conceptus before it can become attached to the uterine wall. The IUD is more widely used abroad and is prescribed by many missionary doctors. The "morning after" prostaglandins are becoming increasingly available in Western countries.

Before 12 weeks the embryo or small fetus can usually be suctioned out into a bottle or pulled out by a curette, a sharp, loop-shaped instrument. A fetus over 12 weeks must often be cut, or crushed by forceps, before being removed.

After 14 weeks the abortionist may stimulate labor by inserting a long needle through the uterine wall to withdraw the amniotic fluid, and then replacing it with a saline solution or another chemical. This "salting out" procedure peels away the skin and usually kills the fetus; but occasionally, one is expelled alive.

A caesarean section operation is usually necessary during advanced pregnancy. Many babies can survive this procedure. Most are deliberately killed in the uterus. Those who should come out alive are suffocated in a plastic bag or drowned in a container of formaldehyde. They are then burned or disposed of in the garbage. Human fetuses have been recovered from dumps in some cities. In Los Angeles the Catholic bishop created a furor by displaying several tiny bodies in a church.

Dr. C. Everett Koop

One of the most concerned evangelical physicians is Dr. C. Everett Koop, surgeon-in-chief of the Philadelphia Children's Hospital. Before the Supreme Court decision in 1973, Dr. Koop predicted that when the U.S. reached a million abortions a year, we would soon also have infanticide. He now claims that infanticide is "being practiced widely in this country today, that is, the deliberate killing by active or passive means of a child who has been born" (*His,* February 1979).

Dr. Koop is editor of the *Journal of Pediatric Surgery,* author of *The Right to Live; the Right to Die,* and co-author of *Whatever Happened to the Human Race?*

During 1979, Dr. Koop and Dr. Francis Schaeffer presented seminars across the United States under the title *Whatever Happened to the Human Race?* In *Life Times,* a study paper prepared for the seminars, Dr. Koop wrote:

There comes a time in the experience of everyone who recognizes the erosion of our human rights, whether in the form of abortion, infanticide, or euthanasia, when he or she says, "What can I do?"

Abortion-on-demand is the keystone of all of the life and death issues which confront the individual concerned about the sanctity of human life. Therefore, as long as abortion-on-demand remains the equivalent of the law of our land, it is to be expected that the recently born and elderly will soon be in the category of nonpersons where the Supreme Court placed the unborn baby (p. 3).

Dr. Koop enumerates four ways in which the abortion decision of the Supreme Court (*Rowe* v. *Wade*, January 22, 1973) can be overturned:

1. In a subsequent ruling, the Supreme Court can reverse its own decision. This is not likely to happen. In several subsequent cases, the Supreme Court has taken an even more hard-nosed stand than in the

original decision to permit abortion on demand.

2. A constitutional amendment could be passed in Congress and then ratified by three quarters of the state legislatures within seven years of the initial passage of the amendment (U.S. Constitution, Article V).

3. A constitutional convention could be called to draft a constitutional amendment which would also need to be ratified by three quarters of the state legislatures.

4. There could be a turnover of Supreme Court justices, replaced by judges who value the sanctity of human life.

Inasmuch as it seems unlikely that the Supreme Court will reverse itself, and in view of the fact that packing in the Supreme Court is also unlikely and a very lengthy procedure, the answer must lie in a constitutional amendment. . . .

Therefore, if the Christian is to have any voice in the recognition of the sanctity of human life, he must get involved personally in the political process of a democracy *(Life Times,* p. 3).

Dr. Koop suggests three ways that you can become involved. First, become knowledgeable, from two directions. You need to know what Scripture teaches about human life, and you need to know the opinions of other people. Second, become affiliated with a national organization. Third, make your wishes known to your senators and representatives.

When you write your lawmakers, letters should be addressed to your own senators and the representative from your district unless you are writing to someone who is running for a higher office or aspires to a higher office in days ahead. The letters should be individualized and should not be a mimeographed form that you sign or a petition that is signed by several people. Use a letterhead, if possible, either personal or business, and type the message. Identify the issue you are concerned about and if you know a senate or house bill number, document your concern with that number. Deal with only *one* issue at a time. Make your points well and be as explicit as possible why you are writing; i.e., how the proposed legislation affects you, your children, your business, your community. The ideal time for such letters to arrive is when a proposed bill is in committee.

Dr. Mildred F. Jefferson

Dr. Mildred F. Jefferson is a general surgeon at Boston University

Medical Center. A graduate of Harvard Medical School, she has received 20 honorary degrees. She is president of Right to Life Crusade, Inc. and is past-president and former chairman of the board of the National Right to Life Committee, Inc.

Life Times editor Randall Nulton interviewed Dr. Jefferson in the fall of 1979.

L. T.: You went to the National Organization for Women Convention in Houston. I imagine some would say you were headed into the lion's den or into the fiery furnace. Why did you go to the NOW convention which obviously was pro-choice and based on the liberal feminist point of view?

M. J.: In the first place, I went because they had no right to have more than five million dollars in federal funds to put on a program which did not reflect the views of the majority of women in this country. I've never seen any kind of sampling of the majority opinion of women in this country to show they support the feminist viewpoint. I also went to Houston to attend the Pro-Family rally which was very well attended. My reason for going as an authority delegate was simply to make that statement, to be visible. The convention was rigged because those who were not feminists had no opportunity to participate in program planning, in spite of their statements to the contrary. I always go where I feel that the soundest interests are either under attack or will have no opportunity to be properly defended.

L. T.: More and more people are finally realizing just what the abortion laws mean. Now they are going to want to know, "What can I do now?"

M. J.: I hope they will remember that basic love and caring concern are the first things that must be evidenced. In a more formal way, they can help with the organizations known as Birthright or Life Line or Birth Care.

People who want to defend their first amendment freedom, can become activists by joining Right to Life organizations. . . .Those who want to move on to the next step must be sure they are active in the political process. . . .

The fight for the rights of life is a people's fight. Our founding fathers recognized that a function and purpose of government is to guarantee those rights that were affirmed in the Declaration of Independence. We consider the most basic of these rights to be the right to life (p. 7).

Louise Matson grew up in Russia, minis-
tered with her husband for 22 years in
Alaska, and presently resides in Califor-
nia. She is involved in teaching children
and in speaking throughout the country.

14
No Guarantees
on Freedom

We live in a world with millions of displaced people who have no place to call home. We live in a world with millions more who suffer oppression mentally, politically and/or physically.

And we cannot ignore the effects of these personal hurts to so many. Nor can we ignore the implications to our own way of life. John Donne's famous line, "No man is an island, entire of itself," was never more evident in the world than in this last quarter of the 20th century.

In recent years, many third-world people have come to North America to make new homes. As they have settled, we have watched them make the personal adjustments necessary to cope with drastic changes.

As political prisoners from Communist countries have escaped or have been exchanged, we have learned more about their former bondage.

Louise Matson sat with me in the restaurant of a little California hotel and told me this story. A motherly, gray-haired lady with fire in her eyes and spunk in her speech, Louise has a deep love for her Lord Jesus. We discussed why, at almost age 65, she was still hard at work on her "part of the wall."

Louise had brought her sister along too and they remarked that they were celebrating an anniversary. It was 51 years ago this month that their family had escaped from Russia.

I was anxious to hear about conditions in Russia, as told by a recent visitor John, but my mind wandered for a few minutes to the first time I had heard Louise tell her "escape" story. We had met at a Bible camp, several years before, where Louise had shared her life and experiences with 150 young campers. For 45 minutes each day, "Aunt Louise" had held them spellbound as she told of a winter escape, soldiers searching houses, and God's miraculous protection over the Klassen family.

Louise Klassen Matson's story is told in more detail in the book *Louise,* written by Margaret Anderson (Shaw Pubs., 1977). She tells about the struggles and changes of one who moves into a new way of life. You too may identify with this. . . .

Louise's Story

You ask me about *rights?* A relative from Siberia has just visited us in Canada. I cannot give you his name or exact details, but I want to share some of the kinds of things that are going on. We will call him John, and you will know that this story is representative of others.

John told me what I've heard before—that in Siberia parents really don't have a right to their children. The government allows a grandma to train them, but the father is sent to a work farm. There are many instances of death by starvation on these work farms. The government, which assigns workers to the farms, considers it one way to control overpopulation. When the husband is gone, the wife also goes to work to accrue "brownie points" to prove the family's "loyalty" to the government.

Our relative John, who was reared in a Mennonite Christian home, told us that he used to believe in God. He said that after his brother-in-law was sent to a farm, his sister had to go to work and build up points for the government. ("Building up the government" is what they call it.) The children were left with her mother. His sister was working too hard, and had too little food, so John called on God. Where was God? John said God didn't hear him, and his sister died. He has her three children to bring up, and John has decided that he will have nothing more to do with God!

John said he has brothers and sisters who still hold to their faith in God, but they must be 'silent believers.' The children are allowed to go to school, where great emphasis is placed on learning to march. (The higher you can kick your legs up in the air while you march, the better Communist you'll make!)

John said he was not really a Communist, but that he turned Communist in order to protect his family. In his profession he could not have earned a living unless he was a Communist. John needed special help for his retarded son, who could not survive in a public school, because he could not march. Now John has retired early so that he gets a pension to exist on.

Reunion in Siberia

More than 40 years ago, my relative adopted John's brother and sister. Having lived much of their lives in Canada, they visited John in Siberia recently after all of those years of separation.

The government allowed them to stay two or three weeks in Siberia, but kept them under constant surveillance. They were given a fabulous, but bugged hotel room.

Other family members came to the hotel to be reunited with their Canadian brother and sister. One sister came whose husband had disappeared. She had been left with five children, and at that time was in such a weak condition that she could hardly walk.

During the reunion, aware that the hotel room was bugged, some were brave enough to just whisper, "We are white on the inside and red on the outside." It was necessary to get along with the government. John said he is thankful that his brother and sister were taken to live in Canada many years ago and were spared this life.

Another of John's sisters has worked to the point of getting a pension of 59 rubles a month, for herself and her children. She and her children are believers in Christ.

Another sister we will call Tina had one cow. (Socialism dictates that no one can have more than one cow until everyone has one cow.) Tina had to deliver the milk to the government, but she stole one glass of milk for each child everyday. Tina had worked for 13 years (from 4 A.M. until late at night daily). When her health finally gave out and she had to quit working, she was told she hadn't worked up enough points to receive any support money for her large family.

This support money is not really comparable to our Social Security, because you are required to work for the government. You must "support" the government with all of your work. When you are in the Work Army, you get no pay, but you build up "points." You are expected to love your country enough to be loyal to it and to work for it. The grandma is there to take care of your children.

Leaving Communism Behind

My aunt and uncle left Russia in 1930 because of Communism. My stepfather had asked them, years before, if they felt Communism was coming. My uncle said that he didn't think it was coming until there was a business meeting where the government told them, "Tomorrow at this time, we want each of you farmers to bring so much money for taxes." My uncle asked where they were expected to get that kind of money, and he was told, "For talking back to me, you will bring twice as much!"

When the meeting was over he went home and told his wife that they were going to sell their horse. This was a horse that he loved more than anything—he was breaking the ties that made Russia his home.

Others in the family sold their farms, and eventually that whole settlement left by train for Germany. A Mennonite was working from the German side to get these people through. But Russia was interfering—my relatives were searched and most of the money they had received for selling their homes was confiscated. However, my aunt had baked a ham and she had hidden their money in the ham bone. (Later, they used this money to buy their children new coats and boots to be worn for school.) Another uncle put his money in the handle of a teapot. They all nearly starved to death en route.

In the meantime, one uncle had to go back to Russia because Grandpa was dying. After he buried Grandpa, he brought Grandma to Germany. The Mennonites sponsored them from Germany to Canada.

Children in Siberia

Today in Siberia when children first start school in kindergarten, the schools teach them that people in all countries except the Communist ones are criminals. They teach that it is wrong to be rich or to have more than you absolutely need. They stress conformity. In school all children wear uniforms—navy blue pants, white shirts, and blazers for the boys; white blouses and navy jumpers for the girls. The children cannot mention God for "there is no such person." It is said that there is religious freedom, but no child is allowed to be in church until age 18 except for weddings and funerals. (These are usually four-hour long services, teaching the Word!) In other cases if a child does go to church, it is in secret.

Russia has child labor without pay. The children harvest potato crops for government distribution. Children are bused to the fields and they stay until the work is finished. The government claims that the children are merely helping to "build the government."

At age 10 the children join Pioneers for Country, with membership signified by a star on their lapels. They march "goose step" around a burning flame which stands for Lenin.

There is emphasis on sports, and lots of chess instruction for the boys. Educationally, the government claims to be ahead of any other country in reading, writing, arithmetic, and science.

One man taught for over 30 years as a math teacher. Because he was a Christian turned Communist, he was singled out to mock Christianity before the students. A Bible was held up and ridiculed. The teachers take the Communist bible and compare it with our Bible, making fun of it verse by verse. Do you think the Holy Spirit can use God's Word, even as it is taught with disdain, to take lodging in young hearts?

Home and Travels

In Russia you cannot choose where you live. You simply live wherever a place is available. John lives with his daughter, her husband, and their three children in a two-bedroom apartment (about 464 square feet, plus bathroom and small porch).

Hospital care is free, but you have no choice of doctor. You must go to whatever doctor lives in your city block. If he or she likes you, it is okay; but if the doctor doesn't, your health care reflects that dislike.

To buy a car, you must be on a waiting list for three to five years, have cash on hand (there is no credit buying), and have a garage with a guard to watch your car.

All land is government-owned and "on loan" to the people. Three fourths of the crops grown are given back to the government. They don't have to tax the citizens because the government just seems to *own* them!

The government takes kids to camps free and fills them with propaganda. Rest camps are provided for everyone at government expense.

No child ever visits another country. Adults can't leave the country without permission from local and federal authorities. You must leave Russia within seven days after obtaining your visa, or not at all. You have a set time to be back in the country, and must report to the embassy at departure and arrival. People who return from travel are afraid to talk, because any positive remark made about another country can result in a prison sentence.

When John visited Canada, he was very afraid of Americans—too afraid even to consider coming over the border into the United States. He was impressed by Canadian roadside rest areas and clean bathrooms, because he had been told we were all very dirty and that there were many slums. When John realized that he was nearing his return to Siberia, he began to shake and his nerves were upset. He took tranquilizers and became like a zombie for the remaining few days of his visit.

Remembering Russia

I remember my own childhood. When I went to grade school in Russia, we had Christian teachers. Our parents hired them to teach us in our German Mennonite villages. A farming community where much grain was raised, our village was located in central Siberia. Several villages like ours were sprinkled across the countryside, with a Russian community close by. I can remember Russian girls coming over to our village inquiring for work. They wanted to learn, and in those days, the Russian families just seemed to let their children grow up instead of training them how to work.

The last teacher I remember was our pastor. One day he received a letter from the government. Lenin had come to power, as the first Communist leader. The letter said that if our pastor would burn the Bible and never mention God in the classroom, he could go on teaching. If he was unwilling, he would be fired. I was there when our teacher received and read that letter. He begged us children to hide much of God's Word in our hearts, because he said worse times were going to come.

When he left the classroom that terrible day, we were broken-hearted children. He had reiterated that worse problems were on the horizon and we were so afraid! The government sent another teacher in his place—a young man trained in the Communist way of life. He told us that there was no God, that our ancestors were swinging in the trees someplace, and that only Russian could be spoken in the school—no more German and Dutch. We began to hate him, to hate school, and to hate our government leaders for what they were doing to us. We had been raised to regard Mom and Dad as law. How could a teacher change everything like this?

Familiar Fears

This fear I felt as a little child of eight or nine gripped me again when I was in my 40s, as a missionary in Alaska. I heard over KICY radio that one woman had persuaded the United States government to take prayer out of schools. I stood and wept before the radio, crying to God, "Take me home! Don't let me go through this once more, dear God!" I just feared what might follow.

Several years ago, while serving at a senior high Bible camp, we heard the announcement that our president had resigned. I felt that sinking feeling again and I went to pieces. I remembered what we had gone through when the Russian czar was overthrown and the new Communist regime was taking over. We were without a leader. I remembered the hunger, the lack of money, and as the heartaches came over me afresh, I wept.

A television was set up in the lodge the next day so that the campers could watch history being made. When the news came that we had a new president, I sat and cried. I felt there was hope and stability, and I thanked God. Remembering that day brings tears to my eyes even now!

As early as 1933, when Roosevelt made the agreement with Russia, I can remember my dad saying, "America needs to wake up before it is too late—things are going the same direction as they did in Russia." I see ominous signs—prayer being taken out of our schools, a president resigning, the government trying to tell parents how they should train their children. This is what I went through in Russia when Lenin finally died and Trotsky took over. He announced that he was going to destroy home life, take the parents and put them into collective farming, and take us kids and put us into institutions. It was all outlined in his first Five-Year Plan.

I have hated five-year plans ever since. When I went to Alaska as a missionary, my first term was to be five years. I reminded them that I had run away from one five-year plan!

Daisy Reflects on Louise's Ministries

For 22 years Louise and her husband worked in Alaska. They lived in a children's home and were parents to as many as 15 children at one time. Aunt Louise made dozens of loaves of bread each week, tucked the children into bed, and mended their clothes. But most of all, she taught them to love and serve Jesus.

After her husband's death, Louise left Alaska. Her heart rebelled at having to leave the children who needed her there, and her prayer was, "Lord, please make me willing and content to stay at home, even when my heart is there!"

In the past decade Aunt Louise has had a ministry throughout America, speaking and sharing her story—her childhood in Russia, the terrifying escape, the journey across China, and the traumatic entrance of the Friesen and Klassen families into America. She tells about her crippled brother who had to stay in China because he could not come into this country unless he could work. She tells of her surrender to Christ, her study in Bible school, and her commission to Alaska.

Aunt Louise has always been committed to the teaching and training of children. When asked about trends or characteristics of parents and children today, she is quick to reply, "It is the terrible indifference of one for the other. Parents don't have time for children. And how I want to tell them that acquisition of *things* is not important. Things can all be taken away overnight—I have seen it happen! Parents must assume the responsibility to train and teach their children and bring them up in the love and nurture of the Lord."

Aunt Louise tells the story of a bright-eyed little boy in one of her audiences who made a burlap wall banner during handwork time. He had cut out the letters for "God Is Good" and had glued them into place—at least, as "in place" as he could put them! Aunt Louise had picked up the completed banner and noticed that the letters had been arranged as only Billy could have imagined:

G O
D I
S G and on the back O O D

Billy beamed, "When I started I didn't know my God was so big!"

Louise Matson serves a *big* God who will not be contained by buildings, banners, or barbed wire. Although semiretired, she works on the staff of a church in California. She teaches several classes of children and only heaven knows how many have been led to trust Christ. Her ample lap accommodates children very easily, and her more than ample supply of LOVE comforts and generously over-flows!

Families Oppressed

However, Louise remembers people like Nina Basilea from Lithuania who has two young children. Her husband Victor is a preacher in an unregistered church. The work he does is forbidden because he witnesses from the depths of the Word of God. He refuses to be censored by the Soviet government.

For years this family has been persecuted. Twenty years ago Victor was told to renounce God in writing. He refused and continued to speak out for God. Job promotions stopped and his pay has been held to subsistent level. Victor and Nina have been declared anti-Soviet individuals.

A short while ago their family was ordered to move out of their home into the street. They were forced to move in with another Christian family in quarters so cramped they can barely exist. Now, the newspapers have begun a slander campaign to turn townspeople against them. An arrest generally follows.

Many times a day, and often in the night Nina gets down on her knees and she prays for her family. School authorities mistreat and ridicule her children. They are forced to attend atheistic club meetings; they come home crying from beatings they have received at school. Continually, she prays that her children will not be taken from her.

In the Soviet Union children are separated from their parents whenever a home is judged to be "unfit." Parental insanity and parental alcohol or drug addiction may be reasons given. Or the government may declare that parents are unfit to raise their children simply because the parents practice a Christian way of life and teach Christian principles in their home!

A mother in the city of Kersk recently lost her two children—a daughter age 4 and a son only 18 months old. What was her crime? Luba Nosova took her children to unregistered worship services. She took them to hear the Gospel!

Last summer a defected Russian pastor reported that 4,000 Christian mothers in the Soviet Union had recently filed an appeal to the Soviet government asking that they be allowed to emigrate with their families. They live in continual fear that their children will be taken from them because their husbands are preaching the Gospel.

Today's Warning

Alexander Solzhenitsyn has repeatedly warned the Western world of the dangers of Communism. In a recent issue of *Time* (February 18, 1980), he again offered "Advice to the West," and spoke of our need to build . . .

Communism is unregenerate; it will always present a mortal danger to mankind. . . . Communism stops only when it encounters a wall, even if it is only a wall of resolve. The West cannot now avoid erecting such a wall in what is already its hour of extremity.

15
Equal Rights Amendment

The November 1978 issue of *Moody Monthly* in a section entitled "The Equal Rights Amendment," focused attention on the proposed amendment to our Constitution. Gary L. Wall summarized its status at that time as follows:

Passed by Congress on March 22, 1972 and sent to the states for ratification, the Equal Rights Amendment (ERA) reads as follows:

Section 1: "Equality of rights under the law shall not be denied or abridged by the United States or by any state on account of sex.

Section 2: "Congress shall have the power to enforce, by appropriate legislation, the provisions of this article.

Section 3: "This Amendment shall take effect two years after the date of ratification."

Within two years, thirty-two states ratified the ERA and passage seemed guaranteed. But as legislative hearings and the application of state-ERA mandated laws exposed its complex nature, progress stalled.

The ERA now has been ratified by thirty-five states, three short of the necessary thirty-eight. Four states—Idaho, Kentucky,

Nebraska, and Tennessee—have voted to rescind their ratification.

The original deadline for ratification was March 22, 1979. But extension has been passed by the House and at press time is being debated in the Senate to give the ERA thirty-nine more months of life until June 22, 1982 (p. 40).

As women have taken sides, vocally defending their viewpoints on this issue, there have been a few surprises.

Wall noted that feminist Eliza Paschall opposes the ERA. The former national secretary of NOW, and founding member of the Atlanta chapter, has changed her position from pro- to anti-ERA. "Mrs. Paschall objects to the ERA because more 'the people who are for it don't agree on what it will mean. You get right back to depending on nine old men.'" She says a study of Georgia laws "revealed that 130 laws would be affected by the ERA. One hundred were already for women. "These protections," she says, "would be lost," (Wall, "Equal Rights Amendment," p. 42).

Anthony Campolo

In his recent book *The Success Fantasy,* sociologist Anthony Campolo points out that the modern woman is psychologically affected by living in a sexist society:

When we call a society *sexist,* we are describing a social system in which females must maintain certain physical attributes and a certain personality style in order to be deemed worthwhile. In such a society, a competent female may be treated like a loser if she doesn't have a pretty face, a proper body shape, and prescribed mannerisms. Lacking these attributes, she may suffer from deep feelings of inferiority, regardless of how bright or efficient she is.

What is worse, she is expected to maintain these desirable physical traits throughout most of her life, even though it is impossible to do so. When she begins to lose her youthful looks, she may feel threatened, particularly if her husband takes an interest in younger women who seem to possess what she has lost (Victor Books, pp. 94-95).

Campolo notes that the feminists, who want the ERA passed, are expressing some legitimate injustices:

It is important for Christians to understand that, whatever their views may be on the constitutional changes sought by the feminist movement, these angry women also represent a righteous indignation against what the modern world does to women. It overtaxes them with impossible role expectations and dehumanizes them by attaching so much of their personal worth to their physical appearance. While Jesus would have rejected some of the claims of the women's liberation leaders, He would have hailed their efforts to end so many of the unnecessary hurts which society inflicts upon modern women (p. 96).

Donald Cole

Donald Cole, pastor of Moody Radio Network, notes that nobody is really sure what may result from passage of the ERA, in terms of indefinite implications (touching areas such as sexually segregated rest rooms). But concern is warranted about the "apparent link between support for ERA and support for other goals which Christians in general find objectionable" ("A Christian Perspective," *Moody Monthly,* November 1978, p. 44). Some of these goals relate to changes in acceptable sexual mores that a Christian cannot condone. He concludes:

If ERA were concerned only with the correction of abuses, it would have more support than it now has. Certainly every thinking person will admit that in few, if any, societies at any time in history have women been given a fair shake.

The Bible calls for mutual submission without respect to sex; and it demands from husbands, at least, a love for their wives patterned after the selfless love of Christ. In addition, there is the idea of protection of women, as opposed to exploitation.

Christian men should take the initiative in seeking legislation designed to protect women from oppressive male domination. Women have legitimate complaints.

In an era in which they are forced to work for a living, or simply choose to do so, they are entitled to just compensation.... Paying a woman comparatively little because she is a woman is a sophisticated (perhaps not so sophisticated) way of cheating her.

Women are entitled to legal protection against husbands who beat them or strangers who assault them on the streets. They are also entitled to a fair shake in the media, meaning a decent portrayal of woman—not as mindless creatures nor as sex objects.

In any case, passage of an Equal Rights Amendment will correct no abuses in a Christian home. For this, new insights into the meaning of Scripture are required. As for society at large, it is unlikely that a new amendment will do what either its supporters or opponents predict.

Equal pay for equal work? The Equal Employment Opportunity Act of 1972 is pledged to get this blessing for women. Access to credit? The Equal Credit Opportunity Act of 1974 secures this right for women. And so it goes.

The new amendment would probably succeed only in tying up the courts in endless litigation. Legislation guaranteeing every reasonable right already exists. If *it* doesn't work, what reason is there to believe that an amendment as vaguely worded as the ERA would do the job?

Betty Friedan

Betty Friedan, author of *The Feminine Mystique* (Norton), is founder of the National Organization of Women (NOW), a group that has considered its first order of official business to be supporting the passage of the ERA. Regarding the language of the amendment ("Dialogue with Betty Friedan," *Moody Monthly,* November 1978, pp. 45-47), she stated:

The ERA is as precise and as unprecise as the Constitution itself. All it says is that the Constitution and the laws of the U.S. shall apply equally to women. How can you be more precise than that?
. . .
I know that ERA will mean that women will not be exempt on the basis of sex from any future draft. And why should they be? Equality of rights and opportunity has got to mean equality of responsibility.

It doesn't mean that mothers or pregnant women are going to be drafted. . . . Even young *fathers* wouldn't be drafted. . . .

Sex discrimination has been permitted in the application of the laws. That would no longer be permissible under ERA. That's all this says.

It does not mean that any fundamental mores will be changed. Private matters not governed by the law or the Constitution are not going to change. . . .

It isn't so much what the ERA will do or won't do—because it won't do all those scary things that the anti-forces are saying—turning women and men into the same genderless species or destroying the family or suddenly making the men stop supporting their wives and forcing women out into the streets. It's not going to do any of those things. It isn't even a matter of what it's going to do because it isn't going to do anthing very dramatic. It is merely going to put that constitutional underpinning under the laws that we've won against sex discrimination, so that they can't be taken away and so that the principle of equal protection of the Constitution is there and the law can be applied to future situations as they arise.

Phyllis Schlafly

Phyllis Schlafly—crusader, leader in the pro-family movement, lawyer, homemaker, mother, wife, author, speaker, debater—is recognized as a prominent Christian opponent of the ERA.

She is fighting ERA ratification because of its potential effect on the family ("Dialogue with Phyllis Schlafly," *Moody Monthly,* November 1978, pp. 44-45). She feels it will "drive the wife out of the home, and it will take away the rights of wives and mothers." Mrs. Schlafly also states:

My major objections can be stated in three parts. First it is a fraud. It doesn't do anything for women. It doesn't give them any rights, opportunities, or benefits that they don't have now. . . .

Second, Section One of the ERA is designed to convert us into a unisex society. It would prevent us from making any distinction between men and women. So the next time we have a war, women would have to be drafted and put in combat just like men. You couldn't have laws that say a husband must support his wife. You couldn't give any preferential treatment to wives, mothers, and widows. You wouldn't be able to make reasonable, common sense separations of treatment such as in single sex schools, fraternities, or athletics; or in other areas such as prison regulations and insurance regulations. . . .

Third, ERA would shift most of the remaining powers of the states to Washington. . . . I think it will bring about fantastic changes, all bad, in our social, economic, and political structure.

*Gladys Dickelman and her husband
Harry are directors of Midwest Conference
Ministries. The mother of two children,
Gladys is the moderator of a Christian
television program. She teaches Bible
classes in her hometown of Barrington,
Illinois.*

16
Demanding Voices
in a
Noisy World

VOICES . . . VOICES . . . VOICES . . . and more VOICES!
So many voices are demanding my attention, my evaluation, and my
response.

Voices of authority . . . voices of doubt. Voices suggesting
appealing alternatives. Voices speaking my own thoughts. Voices
that frighten me . . . some that excite me. Voices telling me what to
wear, to think, to eat.

Voices calling, "Women, this is your time in history to come into
the spotlight, use your power to change this society, and end once and
for all the oppression women have been subjected to through the
rigidity of the patriarchal system."

Voices saying, "The genuine liberation of women encompasses the
power to nurture ourselves and the next generation. If nurturance
means having the economic-political power to provide an environment in which each individual can mature into a unique, open,

trusting, cooperative person, then no woman in patriarchy has the power to nurture either herself or anyone else."

Is this a voice that speaks to you? What woman doesn't want to "mature into a unique, open, trusting, cooperative person"? Voices making this kind of appeal fall on fertile ground, for most women are sensitive to these needs.

Voices are heard through the media—television, radio, newspapers, magazines, and advertising billboards. Bold voices speak through textbooks and teachers in the public schools. The drumbeat of political pressure provides the rhythm for all to join the parade to the new future of human rights, equal rights, children's rights, women's rights, everyone's rights!

Liberation Phobiaitis

Many cultural changes occurred in the 70s, especially as related to marriage, family, religion, sexual mores, the search for love, fulfillment, and identification. We see more and more emphasis placed upon varied escape mechanisms—pleasure, possessions, drugs, alcohol, the occult, or getting caught up in the "esprit de corps" of a movement for social change.

Perhaps the 70s will be remembered as the years of the epidemic of "liberation phobiaitis." People who were unhappy with anything in their lives were susceptible to new alternatives, especially when they identified with what was once known as a very honorable root word, *liberty,* or freedom from undesirable restraints.

In the 70s, we saw an unprecedented rise in the divorce rate even among Christians; we saw family chaos and disrespect for human life—from fetus to old age. Humanistic values which were inculcated into literally every segment of society were the result of direct strategies to accomplish this objective.

Consider some statements written in 1969, and published four years later in *Radical Feminism,* (Anne Koedt et. al., eds., Times Books). Portions from the chapter on "The Feminists: a Political Organization to Annihilate Sex Roles" read:

We seek the self-development of every individual woman. To accomplish this we must eliminate the institutions built on the myth of maternal instinct which prevent her self-development. ...
We must destroy love . . . generally recognized as approval and acceptance. Love promotes vulnerability, dependence... susceptibility to pain ... prevents the full development of woman's human

potential by directing all her energies outward in the interests of others.

Other statements refer to motherhood providing blind approval as a bribe, and to love between husband and wife as a delusion, a self-defense measure developed by the female to prevent her from seeing her powerless situation.

The patriarchal system was described as one which fosters "marriage, heterosex, family, religion and love." Reference is made to "child rearing as the responsibility of all," for children are a part of society.

Sorting Out the Voices

I knew that much of what I was hearing several years ago reflected legitimate hurts, needs, and deep rejection. I had known women who had suffered—yes, for being women! There were women with gifts and abilities, who were literally unsung heroines, yet they were not complaining. Had they simply lost their courage? Were they being willingly "used," happy in always "serving others" without attention or recognition to make them "important and fulfilled"?

I was confused. I wanted to withdraw from the demands of these voices in the world, but it was simply not possible, for they were all around me. They even came from within my own heart and mind, especially when I felt overworked or discouraged with my present full-time role as wife, mother and homemaker. I was being forced to deal with a new dimension of reality in my life and world. I had very strong convictions and values as a Christian woman; yet those voices caused me to begin to ask questions of myself and others, to begin to have doubts about myself and the traditional values I had so willingly followed.

I began to do more reading, to be sure that I wasn't just hearing one particular radical viewpoint. I looked carefully at the issues highlighted in women's magazines. Much of the terminology was new to my vocabulary.

I couldn't go on being naive. As a woman in leadership, I was speaking and teaching others about Christian living. Yet to enter into the real world to which God had sent me, I had to understand that world, and I found I could not understand what was going on in this situation.

With a prayer confessing frustration, I cried out, "Lord, what is this all about? Am I stupid or naive because I am so thoroughly enjoying being a wife and mother? Am I old-fashioned because I believe in sexual honor and purity between husband and wife? Am I prejudiced because I believe that the Bible is truth and is to be our guide for living each day in all of our relationships? Am I foolish because I do not need special recognition for the kindness and love, service and hard work I put forth for my family? Lord, how should I respond to voices of the world?"

A New Mind-Set
Then the Lord gave me what has become a very special verse in my life: "Be still, and know that I am God" (Ps. 46:10, KJV).

What a comfort to know who God is and that what He says is truth—that His plan for me works and is not subject to being changed by voices of temptation in the world. I wanted to settle these issues in my own life, and help other women facing pressures to conform and be sophisticated.

Many young women seek my counsel in personal matters, so I wanted more than superficial answers. I didn't want to live in a vacuum, as I had observed other Christians attempting to do. I resolved before the Lord to be still and know that He was God of my life. His Word would be the lamp for my feet.

Sensing my vulnerability to humanistic voices, I did much soul-searching. I formed convictions based on God's Word, not on the traditions of family, church, or culture. In retrospect I see that God was preparing me, and giving me a heart of compassion.

I am grateful that the Lord does not lead where His grace does not provide. He did lead, and His grace has been sufficient. God was preparing me for what have been the most difficult, depressing, and controversial years of my life. As I look back, I recognize that I literally prayed myself into those hard years!

Outside the Church
It had become apparent to me that a major battle was being waged outside the church, where there was very little opposition. The legislature was enacting laws to which every citizen must submit. As Christians we are specifically commanded to be obedient to the laws of our land and to pray for those in authority over us (see Rom. 13 and 1 Tim. 1—4). I felt that in order to pray and submit effectively, I would have to know what was going on.

I have a favorite passage in 2 Corinthians 5:15-21 which I use as I teach women's seminars. It presents the new life of a Christian as casting aside the old and taking on the new, so that he can be an ambassador for Jesus Christ. The Apostle Paul, in these verses, urges non-Christians to become reconciled to Christ so that they can receive the love He offers. The role of an ambassador according to the dictionary is "an authorized person in residence representing a sovereign power." I had checked that definition on the day that I was wrestling with the Lord about becoming involved in working against the feminist movement. Would I be His ambassador?

Little did I know when I took a stand against the Equal Rights Amendment, believing it to be simply a very bad piece of legislation because of its ambiguity, that such a decision would necessitate more action. Wasn't it enough to tell my friends how strongly I felt, and that they should investigate the feminist movement so that their daughters would not get caught up in it? Doing just that much had caused much consternation within my church and the Bible study group I was teaching. I wondered how much further the Lord wanted me to "stick my neck out."

God chose the "voices" of some Christians—good friends I very much respected—to urge me to attend the Illinois state convention of the International Women's Year. I knew there would be controversy and that the pro-ERA women planned to use the convention as a major thrust to get the Equal Rights Amendment ratified. I was very reluctant to go. It didn't fit into my time schedule, so I decided not to attend.

But God was speaking to me. My husband suggested, "Maybe you should go and find out what is going on." With his confirmation added to my guilt about wanting to avoid controversy, I decided to ask some post-college-age Christian girls and some of the women in the Bible study if they would go with me. If they responded affirmatively, then I would know that the Lord was giving me the push I needed, They did, and a group of us *did* go to the state convention!

Illinois IWY Convention

As I think back to the IWY Illinois and other state conventions, I can say without any hesitation that they were fraudulent, manipulated, illegal, and a disgrace to our country. Five million dollars were appropriated by the federal government to be spent on determining the main concerns of the women. The reality of IWY was that the feminists asked for the money, and then planned all the workshops (including their views on abortion, lesbianism, masturbation, witchcraft) without any input from any of the pro-family (traditional) women leaders. Conferees were treated as "friends or foes" depending on where they stood on the ERA. It became very apparent that the major thrust of the feminists was the ratification of this proposed amendment to the United States Constitution, for they believed it to be the door to their other objectives.

The time came for nominees' names to be placed on the ballot for state delegates to the national convention in Houston. The women from Barrington decided to turn in my name. Chicagoan Nancy Berg, one of the young singles from our group, was also a nominee. Within five hours an incredible thing happened. Our names were circulated on a "hate list;" we were accused of being "enemies of the state, radical right-wingers, members of the Ku Klux Klan, against women's rights," and the delegates were told not to believe us or to vote for us.

My first response to this threat was fear and anger, but we knew our first step was to be still—to know that God was in control. Out on the sidewalk of the Illinois State University campus, we stopped to pray, confessing our fear and anger, and asking God to show us what to do and give us some help.

In less than one minute, the state attorney general walked up to us and asked how the convention was going. I thanked him for his interest and said that we had just prayed for help. We told him of the feminists' domination and of their disgraceful tactics in a convention paid for by our tax dollars. We assured him that the women of Illinois were not fairly represented. We said we would expose the convention as being unfairly manipulated. Viewpoints other than feminism, socialism, and secular humanism were not being given a hearing.

The attorney general assured us that these were most unfortunate and undesirable tactics, and told us there would be a public apology, which there was.

But the tone of the convention remained unchanged. The voting was illegally conducted, particularly the voting on resolutions the final day when a congresswoman from DuPage County asked the parliamentarian to declare that "only those women who were in the spirit of the convention be recognized by the chair." This meant that we who were in opposition to proposals were to be ignored, although we were also official delegates. A final blow came when the congresswoman made a motion to vote on 25 resolutions in one bloc vote, "since the majority of the conferees were in agreement to the major objectives of the convention." This included the "hot buttons" of abortion, ERA, sexual preference, federal control of day-care centers, and more.

When the convention was over, about 300 protesters walked out singing, "God Bless America," and we quickly became organized. There is nothing like a little persecution to shake you from lethargy!

On to Houston!

A bigger jolt for me came the following Tuesday, when I received a phone call saying that I had been elected to be a delegate from Illinois to go to the Houston IWY Convention. After my initial shock, I could only say, "Why, Lord, why me? I didn't know anyone there, at least not enough to be elected. You must have allowed this to happen, but why me, Lord? I don't want it. Am I not doing enough for You? Why do You now have to thrust me further into this mess? Don't You know that I don't have time for anything else? Please Lord? . . . Yes, Lord . . . Thank You, Lord!"

As an elected Illinois delegate to the International Women's Year Convention in Houston (November 1976), I knew that I had to do my homework before and during the convention, and even after returning home. There would be the demands of speaking, debating on radio and TV, and letter writing. Illinois was and continues to be a target state, in that it is the only northern industrial state that has not ratified the ERA. It has been defeated 17 times in our state legislature. Many of our reputable conservative legislators have been targeted for attacks against their reelection if they take a position against ERA or abortion.

In the state conventions, the feminists had organized their followers so that their resolutions had been passed and sent to Houston. The national convention in Houston was the grand finale. After passage in Houston, these resolutions would be sent to the U.S. Congress to be voted into law within six months. (In some cases bills were already in committees ready to be presented to their respective legislative bodies.)

These state conventions had been strategically planned to build momentum and political support, so that when resolutions were written into specific bills, the legislators could be told that women throughout the U.S.—from every state and even the national convention—had voted for these issues. Delegates represented major religious, racial, and geographic areas of each state which added credibility. Every pressure possible was applied to political leaders to support and fund feminist demands.

The culminating national convention, executed with federal money, and promoted by the media, would result in the feminist philosophy becoming one of the major forces of societal change in our nation—changes in marriage, family, economy, values, morals, and educational structures.

Ratification Extension

A major controversary surrounding the ERA since March 22, 1979 concerns the extension time for ratification, The feminists, NOW, and political leaders who had promised their constituencies they would get the ERA ratified, pressured the 95th Congress to illegally extend the time for ratification beyond March 22, 1979 (the deadline contained in the original resolution passed by Congress in 1972).

Phyllis Schlafly leads those opposed to the time extension. She is the national leader of STOP ERA and founder and national president of the Eagle Forum, a conservative organization of politically active women who are committed to the preservation of traditional family values based largely on biblical principles, the U.S. Constitution, and the Judeo-Christian heritage of most citizens.

Mrs. Schlafly is supported in her efforts by former Senator Sam J. Ervin, Jr., professor of law; Jules B. Gerard of Washington University Law School; and many other legal and political leaders. She is suggesting that the federal government has violated states' rights by modifying the language of the amendment which some states have ratified.

Phyllis Schlafly writes in the "Phyllis Schlafly Report," July 1978:
Any attempt to try to change the texts of the 28 state ratification texts in which the March 22, 1979 date was included should make these votes null and void. It would make a laughingstock of Congress to attempt to pass H.J. Res. 638 which is so clearly illegal, and would result in immediate lawsuits. It would be an outrageous piece of federal usurpation for Congress to try to change the language of resolutions passed by the individual states. It would provide further proof that the real goal of the ERA proponents is, as Sen. Ervin says, "to reduce the states to meaningless zeros on the nation's map."

This illegal time extension in 28 of the states would be an excellent issue about which to contact your legislator to influence him and his colleagues to take a firm stand against such violation of states' rights. Congress has literally ignored these states saying, "We the federal government will tell you what you can or cannot do." But the 10th Constitutional Amendment states: "The powers not delegated to the United States by the Constitution, nor prohibited by it to the states, are reserved to the states respectively, or to the people."

Action Not Anger

I want to clarify one point here. I am not merely angry with the feminists for their political activities. I am deeply troubled with the way they have captured the attention of the media and used our tax dollars to espouse their causes. However, I know that if others exercise their political options and I simply stay home and complain, then I deserve to lose. We should be cautious not to criticize others for simply exercising their rights when, in fact, we are doing nothing about the issues.

A danger today is the control of the media by people of similar political views. However, if you request information, the FCC will send you a list of regulations concerning your right to be heard. The "fairness doctrine" allows for all groups in the community to be represented in terms of values and special interests. Many people do not know that this provision exists.

The feminists are using this avenue aggressively. Members of the National Organization for Women formed a NOW FCC Committee in 1972, to assist local chapters of NOW in learning how to apply the FCC regulations. Soon women from NOW were employed by the major networks, working to change future programming in regard to sex roles of men and women, to be in accord with the new standards of NOW.

They influenced TV networks to eliminate any form of sex discrimination in their programming and to include such alternative lifestyles in family structure as lesbianism and homosexuality.

The Equal Rights Amendment had many vocal promoters, until more and more of the women opposing it began to realize that they had rights too.

One day in Chicago, Carol Burnett spoke about her recent pro-ERA involvement. She admitted that she knew very little about ERA, but that she "surely wanted equal rights for her daughters."

Some of my friends who knew their rights under the FCC, called the station and asked for time under the "fairness doctrine" for an opposing viewpoint to be heard. They submitted my name. By noon that day I had received a call from the network asking me to come and be interviewed. I was given free time for the asking to present the opposing position to the ERA, in response to the time Carol Burnett had been given. Sometimes we have not, because we ask not! And we ask not because we have not known what was possible to us!

Strategy

For someone who is serious about exerting a Christian influence on issues in our society, I would suggest using the following strategy:

1. As you define the issues of concern, study the Scriptures and dependable Christian writings relating to the issue.

2. Seek counsel from Christian leaders, including ministers, and professors at Christian colleges and seminaries.

3. Accumulate books, literature, information (including newspaper and magazine clippings) written by the feminists concerning their roots, objectives, goals, and values.

4. Compile a vocabulary and personnel list—"hot button words," legislative terms, strategies, names of leaders, political supporters, media people, and newspaper writers.

5. Subscribe to organizations and periodicals, both pro and con. (The best way to know what a group of people believes is to get the news bulletins sent by the organization's own people.)

6. Develop a card file on issues, so that you can have vital information—statistics, titles, dates of legislation, etc.—at your fingertips. This is a great help in speaking.

7. Multiply yourself by sharing your information and training with someone else. (Students may be very effective workers in writing reports for school on contemporary and controversial issues. Your files will be invaluable for students to do research. All the students I have assisted in writing a report on the ERA have earned an "A" because their research was so complete. Education is essential.)

8. Write letters to the editor dealing succinctly with your concerns.

9. Call in to radio programs that invite you to express your views. You can take advantage of this expensive time!

10. Sign petitions to send to legislators, when applicable.

Beverly LaHaye is a lecturer, radio talk show co-host, and author of How to Develop Your Child's Temperament, *and* The Spirit-Controlled Woman. *She and her husband Tim have four children and five grandchildren. Bev is founder and director of Concerned Women for America, El Cajon, California.*

17

Prayer Is Paramount

"Young lady, from what you have told me, I can see that you are a very selfish woman!" That was the last thing Bev had expected to hear. Here she was—a pastor's wife, mother of four children, a maturing Christian. "You need to ask forgiveness for the sin of self-centeredness."

In 1966, Bev LaHaye had attended a conference, with a heavy and frustrated heart. Seeking some counsel and hoped-for relief in conversation with the speaker, she had been stunned by his observation of her problem.

She says, "I acted on his recommendation, and asked forgiveness, repented of my sin, and the Holy Spirit filled my life. I surrendered to Him the control of my life and future. His cleansing, empowering presence brought with it a deepened sensitivity to sin in my heart. God has been quick to impress upon me those times when I 'get out of line.' "

Bev has authored *The Spirit-Controlled Woman,* which includes lessons God taught her during this building process in her life. (Over

135

one-quarter million copies have been sold!) She has been a college registrar, a radio talk show co-host (on issues affecting the family), and she was awarded the International Youth for Christ *Woman of the Year* award in 1979 in San Diego. Almost 150,000 copies of her book *How to Develop Your Child's Temperament* have been sold.

Concern for the Family

Bev's personal life and ministry have reflected her deep concern for the family from her early days of service. As Bev traveled with her husband, Tim, conducting Family Life Seminars, she met Christian women across the country who were unaware of the extent of government encroachment into family matters. Legislation was being enacted that would affect all of them, as well as their children and grandchildren, but most women were not informed at all, much less involved in making the decisions!

Early in 1977, Bev LaHaye and four other women from San Diego attended a rally and heard the results of the November 1976 International Women's Year meeting in Houston. The recommendations for action were announced, and these recommendations were ready to be presented to the president of the United States.

This report and its implications startled these five ladies because the assumption was made that the report reflected the desires of the majority of American women (women presently comprise 53 percent of the population). Bev was incensed, for these recommendations did not represent her point of view, nor that of the others with her! They discovered that the meeting in Houston had been government subsidized to the tune of $5 million and that the three primary recommendations were: 1) passage of the Equal Rights Amendment; 2) support of federally funded abortions; and 3) the passage of lesbian rights legislation. The five ladies decided they must inform other Christian women.

CWA Is Born

Concerned Women for America was organized in February 1979 to alert women to issues affecting the home and family. Beverly and others have tackled the job of communicating with women because they are convinced that tenets and traditions held dear by many families are being exploited, and often revoked without their consent. Many moral issues are not being given proper coverage by the press and TV newscasts, under the guise of protecting "rights."

Are the rights of our families being threatened? Beverly gives an emphatic YES!

Bev cites the example of the UNICEF-backed International Year of the Child observance. "It is right in there with the ERA in trying to gain control of the family. Children are simply the next step in the scheme, with the central idea being to uphold the rights of the child. The Year of the Child campaign started in the United Nations. It was geared toward the rights of children internationally, and endeavored to remove some of the rights of parents as overseers of the child. Proponents of children's rights view the state as being directly responsible for the child, rather than seeing the parents as responsible for their children, under the state. I disapprove of the removal of parental rights by awarding them to the state."

Even prior to the IYC, Bev took an outspoken stand that involved a risk. In her own community, she had asked how the International Year of the Child would be observed. The superficial information she received compelled her to dig deeper. She discovered that teenagers were being invited to attend meetings in several locations (without parents) to discuss their *rights* under the law.

Bev's interest in the proceedings caused a strong reaction. Someone who attended a planning meeting for the IYC implementation reported that Bev's picture had been held up before the group to identify her as an enemy of children. Those present were instructed not to allow her in any sessions!

Daisy's Findings

I decided to do a little research on my own. Were things really as ominous as Bev was suggesting? A trip to the library and a reading of the controversial book *The Children's Rights Movement* (Beatrice Gross and Ronald Gross, eds., Doubleday) helped me to understand Bev's zeal. I found out that soon after publication Joan Bel Geddes, chief of publications for UNICEF, had offered this book (at a discount) through UNICEF promotion to dozens of organizations and committees involved in IYC planning.

One of the selections in the book is the "Child's Bill of Rights" from Dr. Richard Farson's book, *Birthrights* (Macmillan). He believes these rights are necessary for the liberation of children:

1. The right to self-determination. Children should have the right to decide the matters that affect them most directly.
2. The right to alternative home environments. Self-determin-

ing children should be able to choose from among a variety of arrangements: residences operated by children, child-exchange programs, 24-hour child care centers, and various kinds of schools and employment opportunities.

3. The right to responsive design.

4. The right to information. A child must have the right to all information ordinarily available to adults—including, and perhaps especially, information that makes adults uncomfortable.

5. The right to educate oneself. Children should be able to design their own education, choosing from among many options the kinds of learning experiences they want, including the option not to attend any school at all.

6. The right to freedom from physical punishment. Children should be free from physical threat from those who are larger and more powerful than they.

7. The right to sexual freedom. Children should have the right to conduct their sexual lives with no more restriction than adults.

8. The right to economic power. Children should have the right to work, to acquire and manage money, to receive equal pay for equal work, etc.

9. The right to political power. Children should have the right to vote and be included in the decision-making process.

10. The right to justice. Children must have the guarantee of a fair trial with due process of law, an advocate to protect their rights against the parents as well as the system, and a uniform standard of detention.

Looking Ahead

A 1980 White House Conference on Children is planned, which undoubtedly will be influenced by recommendations from the United States National Commission on the IYC. There will also be a 1981 White House Conference on Families. Beverly and Tim LaHaye are actively involved in Pro-Family Concerns and are praying that President Carter and others responsible for the formation of the family conference will be careful to include those who can speak for the moral concerns of children, and particularly for *parents' rights.*

From the National Organization for Women (NOW) to the United States Congress, there are voices speaking loudly to promote government-sponsored 24-hour day care centers. But one pro-family secular book is a refreshing voice in defense of full-time mothering.

Every Child's Birthright by Selma Fraiberg (Basic Books) offers expert observations regarding some dangers of day care. "When a child spends 11 or 12 hours in the care of indifferent custodians, no parent and no educator can say that the child's development is being promoted or enhanced." Fraiberg further states, "We are living in times when there are voices which denigrate the human family and even cry for its dissolution or its recomposition. I cannot identify the voices of infant psychologists among them."

Fraiberg considers it her professional duty to inform women of the impact their prolonged absence has on their children. If the benefits of long-term day care under *ideal* conditions are dubious, what about the services of many preschool full-day nurseries, which lack expert teachers attuned to the individual needs of each child?

When the five ladies from San Diego formed Concerned Women for America, they set some definite goals. In the beginning they focused on the women of their own city, informing them of moral needs of their nation, urging them to be alert to the dangers of the passage of the Equal Rights Amendment, and warning them about pending legislation as a result of the International Year of the Child. They accomplished this purpose through speaking at coffee parties in homes, at parent-teacher organizations, in government classes in high school, at a variety of women's groups, and in church.

When Concerned Women for America officially incorporated, they established their specific purposes as (1) to inform women of America of the erosion of our historical Judeo-Christian moral standard; (2) to expose movements that are seeking to destroy the family; and (3) to educate women in the principles for living from the Word of God.

Prayer Is Paramount

As more women have become involved in this organization, they have found more work to do because our problems as a nation are many and monumental, ranging from the energy crisis to child abuse. Women everywhere are concerned about the moral issues and the attacks on their families and have been anxious for answers. Bev reports, "We are such an activist-oriented people that our first move was to organize *to do.* But in our organizing to do, we recognized the need of the miracle of God's power to accomplish this overwhelming task." So prayer has been of paramount importance.

Beverly has allowed me to quote extensively from the "Handbook for Prayer Chapters," from Concerned Women for America:

God has given us the secret for dealing with all of the issues confronting America today. This secret is spelled out in 2 Chronicles 7:14 (NIV).

"If My people, who are called by My name, will humble themselves and pray and seek My face and turn from their wicked ways, then will I hear from heaven and will forgive their sin and will heal their land."

Paul substantiates the far-reaching results of the prayers of people in 2 Corinthians 1:11 (NASB).

"You also [will join] in helping us through your prayers, that thanks may be given by many persons on our behalf for the favor bestowed upon us through the prayers of many."

Apparently God has chosen to act on our behalf through the prayers of others. In 1 Timothy 2:2 we are asked to pray for authorities in government that we might lead a tranquil lifestyle.

Concerned Women has determined that prayer will be our priority as an organization, and we are inviting women across our nation to join with us in launching prayer chapters in local communities.

Concerned Women for America is attempting to promote across the country prayer chapters composed of prayer chains who pray daily for those in authority in the individual states and for our nation. If we had only one chapter in each state, our 100 senators would be prayed for everyday. By praying specifically for each senator that God would direct him in his vote, we can expect changes in government! Praying by name for each member of the Supreme Court and the individual case before the Court will result in freedom preserved for our country through our judicial system. Every appointment our president makes could be bombarded by prayer to God for a right selection. We believe we could begin to see righteousness exalting our nation.

Key 16

To encourage prayer for leaders in government, CWA borrowed the idea of a Key 16 prayer list from Support for Action of Garland, Texas. We all have 16 people in our country who make decisions that affect our lives and the lives of our children.

If you do not know the name of your congressman, the post office has this information and the office of the district clerk has the names of state senators and state representatives.

God delights to use the Bev LaHayes of the world—and you and me—as we work for Him. And He listens when we pray!

KEY 16 Prayer List

"Prayers, intercessions, and giving of thanks be made for . . . all who are in authority, that we may lead a quiet and peaceable life in all godliness and reverence" (1 Tim. 2:1-2).

U.S. Government Five

President	1600 Pennsylvania Avenue Washington, D.C. 20500
Vice President	Executive Office Bldg. Washington, D.C. 20501
Senator	
Senator	
Congressman	

State Government Five

Governor	
Lt. Governor	
Attorney General	
State Senator	
Assemblyman	

Local Government Six

Mayor	
City Councilman	
City Attorney	
School Board Member	
County Supervisor	
Sheriff	

*Norma Gabler and her husband Mel
founded Educational Research Analysts
in Longview, Texas. Norma is a mother,
homemaker, speaker, and writer. She was
awarded the Texas good citizenship med-
al (Sons of the American Revolution), the
Texas Senate Award of Appreciation, and
the Texas Merit Mother Award.*

18
Called to
Constructive
Criticism

". . . And tell Norma I will be praying for her!" I hung up the
telephone after a lengthy cross-country call. Now I knew more than
ever that Norma Gabler was a special lady, and I could hardly wait to
meet her. Mel Gabler had spent a good chunk of time bringing me up
to date on his gregarious wife. She was away on a brief R and R, to
recover from minor foot surgery before another national magazine
planned "a day with the Gablers" in preparation for an upcoming
issue. And the "Sixty Minutes" TV program was soon to be aired
featuring the Gablers and their crusade to improve school textbooks.

A Son's Challenge
Norma is now grandmother to four, but the story of Norma and Mel
Gabler's involvement in education began 20 years ago when their son
Jim challenged his parents to read and react to his history textbook
from a Texas high school.

"Dad, what did the founders of our nation intend to accomplish when they wrote the Constitution?"

Mel told him that they tried to establish a government which would be strong enough to unite the people, but which would leave them as much of their God-given freedom as possible, with most of the governing left up to state and local governments.

Jim said, "Not according to my book."

Handing Mel the book, he opened it to the chapter on the Constitution and showed 10 subheads about the Constitution, of which 2 concerned governmental powers. One of these enumerated powers granted the new government and the other listed limitations on the states. There was nothing about any restrictions on the federal government and nothing about rights or freedoms retained by the people and the states. This set Mel on fire.

He passed the book to Norma and she too became very upset. They looked further in this and in other history texts obtained from friends. Familiar stories and sayings of patriots were missing. In most they could not find Nathan Hale's "I only regret I have but one life to lose for my country." Nor Patrick Henry's "Give me liberty or give me death." Leaders like George Washington seemed to be downgraded. There was only a brief sentence in one book about the loyalty of his army at Valley Forge and nothing about his deep religious faith (Hefley, *Textbooks on Trial,* Victor Books, p. 15).

What's Your Motivation?

I thought back to my phone conversation with Mel . . . .

"Mel, can you tell me just what it is that you and Norma are willing to fight for—why you and Norma have made this textbook scrutiny a focus of your lives, even a ministry?"

"We are Christians, Daisy, and we love our country. We realize that in this nation there is a terrible trend away from God, particularly in education. One generation after another is being exposed to the atheistic religion called *humanism.*

"We could never have imagined the path that the Lord would take us down. We are in this work today simply because every time we have tried to quit, God has pushed us back into the fight!"

Back in 1961 Mel and Norma had called into a widely heard radio talk show to share some of their concerns about the textbooks. They mentioned the absence of information that was so important to the broad spiritual base upon which America had been founded. The textbooks also seemed to have left out the three Rs and emphasized "values clarification" too much. All parents are interested in their children developing a value system, but Norma questioned whether Christian parents want their children's values shaped by a humanistic course of study. The textbooks concentrated on *changing* attitudes and *changing* values, presumably *away from* those learned at home and *toward* other values and attitudes.

For a period of time, they called this talk show at least once a week; finally, the station manager invited Mel and Norma to a hotel for a special meeting. They talked at length with the emcee of the talk show, and then he calmly announced to them, "Well, folks, you are my show tonight!"

On the Air

The Gablers were not public speakers, although both had been very active in their church and Sunday School. Mel was a clerk in the office of an oil company and Norma was a wife, mother of three sons, and homemaker. The idea of being on the radio was not entirely appealing to them. Anyone could call in to ask questions and the Gablers felt inadequate to give the answers.

But they did appear on the show. And today Mel and Norma testify to the fact that the Lord gave them unusual ability during that one and one-half hour program to communicate ideas and facts that even they didn't realize they knew so well.

They basically shared quotes from textbooks—about 20 pages' worth that had been gleaned by an organization called Textbooks for America. The response was tremendous. They couldn't keep up with the inquiries. People were asking: "What can we do about it? You seem to have the problem under control in your area, but what about us? Help us!"

A sympathetic printer duplicated 1,000 copies of those 20 pages for them and he asked Mel and Norma if they could collate the booklets themselves.

"Collate?" Mel had not the foggiest notion what *collate* meant. The printer arranged the piles of pages on a round table, and led Mel and Norma and one of their sons around it, picking up the pages. Then the printer went home.

All night long the eager threesome went around in circles, assembling 1,000 pamphlets (20,000 sheets of paper), and these pamphlets were quickly distributed. So many concerned parents and educators used this information that more copies were needed. The process was repeated for another 1,000.

Hard Work in the Country

On the phone I had asked Mel about his family and what values he and Norma had tried to instill in their own sons.

"The best thing we ever did for our family was to buy a 68-acre farm in Hawkins, away from town. Our son Jim would sometimes come home from school frustrated because of his lack of interest and ability in sports (which seemed to be the prime emphasis for school spirit and popularity), feeling insecure in his relationships with other students, or maybe just whoppin' mad at his brothers. I would put him on the tractor, send him out to the fields, and in 15 or 20 minutes he would be singing at the top of his lungs. The best therapy I can think of is hard work! Yes, lots of parental interest, hard work, and vigorous training were our tools in shaping the values of our boys. Two are computer scientists now.

"We gave them all bucket-fed calves. Do you know what that is? When a calf is taken from its mother, it needs to be fed from a bottle or a bucket with a nipple in it. Each of the boys had to get up early to feed his calf before he went to school at 7:30, and it didn't hurt him a bit. Each boy's calf was his responsibility." Mel and Norma guided their children in practical ways.

Moving to the farm provided an educational advantage as well. "Before, we had lived in a town where a boy student's academic achievement was secondary to his athletic accomplishments. I can remember our son coming home with an average or below average report card (when we knew he could do better) and saying to us, 'Mom and Dad, only squares make good grades.' There seemed to be no incentive at all. In contrast, we will always be grateful to the Hawkins High School that did promote and encourage academic excellence."

Jim's Testimony

Son Jim was the one who started the Gablers' involvement with textbooks and trends in education. Jim himself was invited to testify in 1962 before the Texas State House of Representatives Committee on the choice and evaluation of textbooks. He stayed up preparing until 2 A.M. in order that every word be his own when he was called to speak before the committee.

Jim testified that he represented only himself, as a high school student currently studying the one American history textbook used in his school. He cited chapters that puzzled him, such as the Revolutionary War section:

"I have always thought George Washington one of our greatest patriots. After studying him in this book, I was left with the impression that Washington did little more than Baron von Steuben or Benedict Arnold.

"My earlier American history textbooks had a picture of Washington at Valley Forge as he was praying to God. I believe this to be a great piece of art since it shows George Washington's faith in our Father in heaven. I have yet to find such a picture in this book."

He expressed concern that the book was unbalanced in its coverage of Constitutional provisions in that it didn't mention any *limits* set on the power of the federal government. Refuting previous testimony which had called the book "only a tool," he stated:

"This is definitely not true. My teachers use the book as the final authority. I was not even allowed to elaborate on a world history test last year. The teacher told me that I was to put only what was in the book or it would be counted wrong. Does this sound like the book is only a tool? It doesn't to me."

Not as Simple as It Sounds

The Gablers recall that they had much to learn at the time they began gathering textbook information. "In the beginning it was very hard for us to find out anything. We were greenhorns in this business of challenging the intelligentsia and daring to criticize *experts*. We had always considered those in the field of education to be so much more knowledgeable than we were.

"When we assembled our first sheet of information, we sent it out to our Christmas card list of friends and relatives, thinking for sure that once they became aware of what was happening, our job would be done. We were confident that each of them would act in his own situation—the only thing people lacked was the information! *Don't you believe it!*"

Archibald Roosevelt, son of President Theodore Roosevelt, wrote to Mel Gabler. Mr. Roosevelt, himself a researcher and strong supporter of free enterprise, suggested, "Mel, don't try to win the majority. All victories are won by dedicated minorities."

A point of discouragement for the Gablers right now is the great number of people who win one small battle in the effort to improve textbooks, and lose the war! It is the persistent, continuing effort which produces results. The Gablers have earned success and respect because they have worked hard and done their homework. They have persevered in their building on the assigned part of "the wall."

A Right to Speak

When Mel was transferred to Longview in 1965, Mel and Norma's growing library went with them. Several rooms in their new home were devoted to office and bookshelves, and Norma regularly attended the hearings on textbooks for Texas at the State Board of Education meetings.

In one meeting, the board considered the book *Economics for Our Times*. It was evident to Norma that this book leaned toward a government-controlled economy, as did four other books under consideration. She was incensed at the lack of response by the board members. In addition, when she stood to speak, one of the board members challenged her right to testify. Norma stood and spoke boldly:

"You ask me about my qualifications. Let me tell you. First, I am a mother of three sons. Second, I am a taxpayer whose money pays for these books. Third, I am a registered voter, who by law you represent. Can you think of three better reasons?"

A smiling nod of approval from the other members of the board encouraged her to go on with her speech.

From its inception, the Gablers have personally invested heavily in their project. Textbooks are expensive. There are printing and transportation costs, phone bills, and they have hired office help to handle the increasing work load. Norma has had hundreds of invitations to speak to groups, to write articles, and to share findings with people in all parts of the country. There is such a great impact when a textbook is held up and read from directly, that much of the available money has gone into the purchase of books.

Government Control

In the early 1960s the federal government had very little input into education. Perhaps it was just after Sputnik that Americans began to voice concern about how much more advanced Russian education seemed to be. Our government began to pour billions of dollars into education, primarily through the Health, Education, and Welfare Department.

In September 1979, a National Department of Education was established, providing another cabinet post and thousands of jobs to be supported by the taxpayer. And what the government subsidizes, it must control.

Mel and Norma are concerned for education and they fear any trend that gives the federal government more influence or control over American lives and families. A federally standardized curriculum would allow concerned people like the Gablers very little supervision of local education and textbooks.

Based on his study of American history, Mel defines a *conservative* government as one that believes in acting by established procedures, making changes based on previous experiences and bringing about those changes voluntarily, whereas a *liberal* governmental philosophy makes innovations quickly and forces changes on citizens. We have a choice of experience vs. experiment, or trial vs. tradition. Mel and Norma feel that we can't afford to educate our children by trial and error, as was discovered in the system of New Math.

Is it proper for the federal government to grab control, little by little, of the educational system of our country? To disallow parents, even local school boards, the right to supervise their children's education? Norma Gabler feels it is not right. She travels back and forth across this country championing in a low-key but determined way, the rights of parents to act with responsibility in education.

There are countless places in America where parents do not have the right to speak before textbooks are chosen. And often where input is possible, very few parents are interested enough to read and evaluate the books before they are adopted.

Christians Made Aware

Sometimes Christians are simply unaware of the subtle secular influence in school textbooks. In Florida, a certain lady had been a schoolteacher for 29 years. She also wrote curriculum materials for a Sunday School publishing house and started a children's Christian newsletter, to send to children within her own acquaintance and to those on her Christmas card list. "Bread for Children" became so popular that thousands of parents asked to have their children on her mailing list! Norma Gabler remembers the first time this teacher contacted her:

"I am astounded by reading your book, *Textbooks on Trial,* and I have taken time and done research through the books that I have used in my classroom over these years in elementary school. Norma, I have been teaching a *humanistic* philosophy, and at the same time teaching Sunday School to some of the same children. I have come to the realization that I have been doing more damage in school during the week than I could ever hope to undo in one hour on Sunday morning! If I had only known!"

An American teacher working for the government in Germany wrote to Norma. "Periodically, we receive new textbooks and I have had the strangest experience. Several of them have been seemingly impossible for me to study and then translate into teaching. I have prayed consistently that the Lord would guide everything that happens in this classroom. Now that I have developed a discernment to humanism, I realize that my difficulty in teaching this material is a check of the Holy Spirit. God is faithful to provide wisdom!"

Many Christians are so involved in church activities that they don't take time to pursue these issues. Some are not aware of government intrusion into school curriculum or they do not know what they can do. The Gablers and their staff can advise others on how to become involved and effective. Their state of Texas will spend about $45,000,000 on textbooks for public school use during each of the next five years. Norma and Mel and their staff are right in there poring over textbooks and daily furnishing information to concerned citizens.

Norma has won many prestigious awards for parental leadership and her contribution to education. She and Mel have appeared on nationwide television and have been featured in national magazines. Norma has spoken from coast to coast about school textbooks, and she plans to continue her involvement in textbook review.

Norma Gabler is a pacesetter. But she is quick to say that simple honesty and hard work, in the power of God, are the reasons for her success. All concerned Christians can build on "the wall."

Building Blocks You Can Place

Abortion

1. The Christian Action Council, 788 National Press Building, Washington D.C. 20045.

2. National Committee for a Human Life Amendment, Phone: 202-785-8061.

3. Crusade for Life, P.O. Box 1433, Whittier, California 90609.

4. National Right to Life Committee, Inc., 529 14th St., N.W., #314, Washington, D.C. 20045.

5. Ad Hoc Committee in Defense of Life, Inc., 8810 National Press Building, Washington, D.C. 29945.

6. American Citizens Concerned for Life, 6127 Excelsior Blvd., Minneapolis, Minnesota 55416.

7. Americans United for Life, 230 N. Michigan Ave., #515, Chicago, Illinois 60601.

8. U.S. Coalition for Life, Export, Pennsylvania 15632.

9. Central Office, Alternatives to Abortion International, World Federation of Pro-life Emergency Pregnancy Service Centers and Helplines, Hillcrest Hotel, Suite 511, Toledo, Ohio 43699. (This group offers many local services in communities.)

Displaced Peoples

1. Seek ways to minister to displaced peoples who come to our country.

2. Use your influence and vote to protect our religious freedom.

3. Prepare your family for the possibility that they could someday lose their freedoms.
    4. Additional resource:
        Evangelism to Communist Lands, Box 303, Glendale, California 91209 (in Canada, Box 65899, Vancouver, B.C. V5N 5L3).

Family Concerns

    1. Make a prayer list according to the Key 16 pattern, for people influencing your life in politics.
    2. Join with at least two others to pray regularly for those people.
    3. To become more aware of pro-family people in your area and constructive action you could take, contact organizations such as the National Pro-Family Coalition on the White House Conference on the Family, and Concerned Women for America.
    4. Use Gladys Dickelman's suggestions and sources of information in chapter 16.
    5. Additional resources:
        Concerned Women for America (Beverly LaHaye, National Director), P.O. Box 20376, El Cajon, California 92021.
        Christian Citizens Alert, monthly newsletter published by Midwest Conference Ministries, Inc., 118 Barrington Commons, Suite 216, Barrington, Illinois 60010, to serve Illinois. Copies available for church distribution.
        Illinois Eagle Forum, Box 112, Morton, Illinois 61550. ("The Phyllis Schlafly Report").
        National Pro-Family Coalition on the White House Conference on the Family, 418 C Street, N.E., Washington, D.C. 20002.
        Pro-Family Forum, P.O. Box 14701, Fort Worth, Texas 76117.
        Evangelical Child and Family Agency, 127 N. Dearborn St., Chicago, Illinois 60602.

Public Schools

1. Take an active part in your child's school PTA.

2. Find out the procedure for textbook selection in your district. Write to the Gablers for helpful information.

3. Read books on this subject, such as *Textbooks on Trial* and *For Such a Time as This.*

4. Follow these suggestions for making changes in the textbooks used in your schools:

• Become involved in the adoption process, because removing a book that has already been purchased is almost impossible.

• Speak to school board members (perhaps one at a time) about your views prior to any public meetings.

• Use the book in question itself when you present your views. Do not rely on a review you have read or a secondhand opinion.

• Use tact. Earn respect and be consistent.

5. Additional resource:

Educational Research Analysts (Mel and Norma Gabler), P.O. Box 7518, Longview, Texas 75601.

Prayer

1. *Intercessors for America Newsletter,* voluntary contribution, monthly—P.O. Box D, Elyria, Ohio 44035.

2. *United Prayer Ministries,* Evelyn Christenson, Founder, 4265 Brigadoon Dr., St. Paul, Minnesota 55112.

3. *The Church around the World,* listing concerns for prayer. Tyndale House Publishers, 336 Gundersen Drive, Wheaton, Illinois 60187.

SECTION IV

WHO WILL SPEAK UP FOR RIGHTS?

IRENE CONLAN is a political organizer, teacher, and wife of a former congressman.

LINDA RANEY WRIGHT takes her Christian convictions to secular college campuses to give students a Christian perspective on subjects they are studying.

MARTHA ROUNTREE is involved in leadership training in the nation's capitol.

TRUDY CAMPING speaks up for Christian concerns as a state senator.

SARAH MADDOX is a homemaker committed to challenging others to involvement.

Nehemiah said, "You see the trouble we are in: Jerusalem lies in ruins, and its gates have been burned with fire. Come, let us rebuild the wall of Jerusalem, and we will no longer be in disgrace. . . . The God of heaven will give us success." Nehemiah 2:17, 20, NIV

19
Humanism

In one form or another the concepts upon which humanism is built have generated problems from man's beginnings—the self-sufficiency of man apart from God is not a new idea. But many people see this century as the "humanist century." Interest in and study of humanism is mushrooming. The January 1979 issue of the *Freeman Digest* was devoted to material about the Aspen Institute for Humanistic Studies, a world-wide organization conducting advanced seminars in global ideology and humanistic studies, where possible plans for the future of humanity are considered.

The institute is a:

continuing effort to help shape a world in which there is individual freedom, creativity, and fulfillment as well as social justice. . . .

The institute is independent, international, nonpartisan and nonprofit. It considers contemporary issues from a human-centered viewpoint . . . is managed by a leadership determined to perpetuate the integrity of the Aspen Institute idea; and it is supported by diverse foundations, tuition, individuals, corporations and, to a smaller extent, by grants from national and international public organizations (official pamphlet, Aspen Institute for Humanistic Studies, New York).

155

Its central office is in New York City and it has centers of activity in Maryland, in Aspen, Colorado and in several other states, as well as in Berlin, Tokyo, and Hawaii. It conducts seminars on Asian thought and has begun a Latin American program.

The late John D. Rockefeller, III called the present period of transformation emerging in the United States the Second American Revolution. He wrote:

As for the content of this movement, it seems to me most expressive and accurate to refer to it as a *humanistic* revolution, for it springs from the first source of change mentioned above—the wants and needs and aspirations of people. It embodies a desire to create a person-centered society, to harness the forces of economic and technological change in the service of humanistic values. Its vision is that the ideals and purposes that give life its higher meaning may now finally be within our grasp.

To use the dictionary definition of humanism, this revolution is characterized by a "devotion to human welfare, interest in or concern for man." It is a search for "a doctrine, set of attitudes, or way of life centered upon human interests or values." I believe this is very much in the directions perceived by Revel and Reich. A true revolution, Revel wrote, is a "social, cultural, moral, and even artistic transformation, where the values of the old world are rejected, where relations between social classes are reconsidered, where relations among individuals are modified, where the concept of the family changes, where the value of work, the very goals of existence are reconsidered."

The word "revolution" is overworked, particularly in the advertising world, but it is important to realize that what is being considered here is revolution in the real sense. (*The Second American Revolution*, Harper and Row, pp. 4-6).

The principles of humanism have been identified by the prominent humanist philosopher Corliss Lamont, a graduate of Harvard and Columbia Universities and later an instructor at Cornell, at Harvard and Columbia Universities, and at the New School for Social Change. In 1965 he published a revised and enlarged version of *The Philosophy of Humanism*, in which he cites 10 central propositions of the humanist philosophy:

Naturalistic Metaphysics

First, Humanism believes in a naturalistic metaphysics or attitude toward the universe that considers all forms of the supernatural as myth; and that regards Nature as the totality of being and as a constantly changing system of matter and energy which exists independently of any mind or consciousness.

Man Is an Evolutionary Product

Second, Humanism, drawing especially upon the laws and facts of science, believes that man is an evolutionary product of the Nature of which he is part; that his mind is indivisibly conjoined with the functioning of his brain; and that as an inseparable unity of body and personality, he can have no conscious survival after death.

Ultimate Faith in Man

Third, Humanism, having its ultimate faith in man, believes that human beings possess the power or potentiality of solving their own problems, through reliance primarily upon reason and scientific method applied with courage and vision.

Human Beings Possess Genuine Freedom of Choice

Fourth, Humanism, in opposition to all theories of universal determinism, fatalism, or predestination, believes that human beings, while conditioned by the past, possess genuine freedom of creative choice and action, and are, within certain objective limits, the masters of their own destiny.

All Human Values Grounded in This Earthly Experience

Fifth, Humanism believes in an ethics or morality that grounds all human values in this-earthly experiences and relationships and that holds as its highest goal the this-worldly happiness, freedom, and progress—economic, cultural, and ethical—of all mankind, irrespective of nation, race, or religion.

Continuous Self-Development

Sixth, Humanism believes that the individual attains the good life by harmoniously combining personal satisfactions and continuous self-development with significant work and other activities that contribute to the welfare of the community.

Development of Art and Beauty

Seventh, Humanism believes in the widest possible development of art and the awareness of beauty, including the appreciation of Nature's loveliness and splendor, so that the aesthetic experience may become a pervasive reality in the life of men.

Far-Reaching Social Programs

Eighth, Humanism believes in a far-reaching social program that stands for the establishment throughout the world of democracy, peace, and a high standard of living on the foundations of a flourishing economic order, both national and international.

**Complete Social Implementation of Reason and
Scientific Method**

Ninth, Humanism believes in the complete social implementation of reason and scientific method; and thereby in the use of democratic procedures, including full freedom of expression and civil liberties, throughout all areas of economic, political, and cultural life.

Unending Questioning of Basic Assumptions

Tenth, Humanism, in accordance with scientific method, believes in the unending questioning of basic assumptions and convictions, including its own. Humanism is not a new dogma, but is a developing philosophy ever open to experimental testing, newly discovered facts, and more rigorous reasoning. (Corliss Lamont, *The Philosophy of Humanism,* Frederick Ungar Publishing Co., pp. 11-14).

Secular humanists reject the concept of a personal, active God:

In the meaningful perspectives of the Humanist philosophy, *man,* although no longer the darling of the universe or even of this earth, stands out as a far more heroic figure than in any of the supernaturalist creeds, old or new. He has become truly a Prometheus Unbound with almost infinite powers and potentialities. For his great achievements, man, utilizing the resources and the laws of Nature, yet without Divine aid, can take full credit. Similarly, for his shortcomings he must take full responsibility. Humanism assigns to man nothing less than the task of being his own saviour and redeemer. (Lamont, *Philosophy of Humanism,* p. 283).

Concerning the existence of God, The *Humanist Manifesto II* states:

We believe, however, that traditional dogmatic or authoritarian religions that place revelation, God, ritual, or creed above human needs and experience do a disservice to the human species. Any account of nature should pass the tests of scientific evidence; in our judgment, the dogmas and myths of traditional religions do not do so. ... We find insufficient evidence for belief in the existence of a supernatural. ... As nontheists, we begin with humans not God, and with nature not deity.

And with regard to life after death and man's need of salvation by God it states:

But we can discover no divine purpose or providence for the human species. While there is much that we do not know, humans are responsible for what we are or will become. No deity will save us; we must save ourselves. . . .

Promises of immortal salvation or fear of eternal damnation are both illusory and harmful. They distract humans from present concerns, from self-actualization, and from rectifying social injustices. . . . There is no credible evidence that life survives the death of the body. . . .

In Summary

Many of the goals of humanism seem valid and worthwhile. The dignity and value of man is stressed, and humanists are deeply committed to the welfare and improvement of society. However, we as Christians must reject the system because it is built upon a foundation which is overtly opposed to the Christian God, as revealed in Jesus Christ and in the Scriptures.

Irene Conlan, nurse, mother, and wife of former congressman John Conlan, is active in the political scene. She serves as president of the Scottsdale, Arizona Republican Women. Irene is author of the book Women, We Can Do It!

20
Send Your Finest into Government

While working as director of nursing at St. Luke's Hospital in Phoenix, Irene was hostess one evening at a hospital Christmas party, where she met a handsome young state senator, John Conlan. They were married in 1968, in the midst of John's third campaign for the Arizona State Senate seat. Son Christopher was born during the fourth campaign, and second son, Kevin, was born two days after John's election to the United States House of Representatives!

Irene's Story
1972—and John was in Congress. Exploring my new world, I began to realize that some significant legislation was being passed which would have a critical impact on the Christian community. I could see the trends toward more liberal and humanistic philosophies. My husband and I realized that some leaders and certain pieces of legislation aimed to render ineffective the Christian community. The message of salvation apparently presented a threat to some in influential leadership, and they wanted to hinder the proclamation of the Gospel of Jesus Christ.

Because I was the wife of a very articulate Christian congressman, I was frequently asked to speak in public meetings. As I traveled, sharing the political issues and trends with women in our land, I found that few understood what was happening or what they could do to make a difference. They read the newspapers but did not relate the news to themselves personally, or to the Christian community.

After a speaking engagement for the Greater Los Angeles Sunday School Convention, Fritz Ridenour of Regal Books asked if I would be willing to put my thoughts down on paper. As I prayed and thought about his suggestion, I realized that this was the perfect opportunity to let women know what they could do to help.

As I researched such issues as the problem in education, relativism in morality, permissiveness, and women's liberation, I kept coming across the words *humanism* and *humanists*. I found out that humanism had been declared a religion by the United States Supreme Court.

I obtained a copy of the *Humanist Manifesto,* and I discovered that this has been the bible of the Humanists. Published first in 1933 and written mainly by John Dewey, it was republished in 1973. After studying this document, I realized that most Christians know nothing about the *Humanist Manifesto*—pastors, key Christian leaders, women, mothers—and yet this philosophy has a tremendous impact on our lives.

Humanists aggressively pursue their goals and intend to reach them. They are well-organized into ethical societies rather than churches, and their basic goal is to reach the minds of our children and give them the opportunity to become humanists. The final goal of humanism is world socialism.

As I became familiar with some of the indicators of humanism, I found evidence of it everywhere in our society.

Humanism in Education
There has been a tremendous change in public education in the past 30—40 years. While not every school system is permeated with humanism, all are affected, since schools use the same textbooks across the country with little variation from district to district. School programs such as MACOS (an acronym for *MAN: A Course of Study*) expose children to new cultures and seem to condone their moral practices that have been traditionally frowned upon in the United States. I find some of the exercises utilized in this course appalling! And yet, it is being taught in 1,700 schools.

The story of how this program came into being is really very shocking. An English socialist named Breuner devised this program, through our publicly funded National Science Foundation. When he took the program to textbook publishers, they turned it down, believing the American public would never accept this kind of program. He went back to the National Science Foundation and asked Congress for more funding, obtained it, and set up his own publishing company. He then offered MACOS at a subsidized rate to all the school districts in the country. Bearing the seal of approval from the National Science Foundation and being sold at a reduced rate, MACOS looked very good to the public school systems and they bought it. What a travesty—our tax money paying for something that can drastically alter our children's moral values!

Also, in the public school system, we have such programs as values clarification incorporated in each course, designed to encourage children to make their own moral and value judgments—seemingly something we would all want for our children. But, in actuality, the goal of this program is to make the student unlearn what he has learned at home about morals. The child is guided in making value judgments in a group situation, based on the lowest common denominator and stressing situation ethics. Christian absolutes may be undermined.

An outgrowth of secular humanism is permissiveness—doing what makes you "feel good." According to the humanist, there is no right or wrong.

We affirm that moral values derive their source from human experience. Ethics are autonomous and situational, needing no theological or ideological sanction. Ethics stem from human need and interest. To deny this distorts the whole basis of life. Human life has meaning because we create and develop our futures. Happiness and the creative realization of human needs and desires, individually and in shared enjoyment, are continuous themes of humanism (*The Humanist Manifesto II*, Ethics, Prometheus Books).

There are men and women in the United States Congress who are avowed humanists, while others are not aware of humanism and its threat, and therefore do not have the tools to oppose its influence. There are humanists in the school system, and even in the clergy, as incongruous as it seems!

It was after I began to realize the influence of humanism and the impact of those who subscribe to its doctrine, that I became motivated to combat it.

What Can One Person Do?

Irene Conlan wondered what she could do. She saw in our society a general deterioration of our moral strength, with negative and destructive symptoms emerging more visibly. She searched for ways Christians could make contributions in the midst of this confusion.

Right now Irene is working in Arizona. John Conlan is a precinct committeeman. In the past, he served in the United States House of Representatives from Arizona. John and Irene are willing for him to return to Congress if the Lord opens the door.

Irene is a deputy registrar for their area. She spends a good deal of time registering people to vote—as many as she possibly can! Many of her acquaintances are Christians; she is signing them up.

Irene serves as president of the Scottsdale Republican Women. Their goals include getting information out to the community, and seeing good people elected to public office. It is a very active group, and Irene encourages more Christians to become involved in this avenue also.

What Should the Christian Do?

There are supposedly more than 40 million born-again believers in this country. But the Christian community, by and large, does not vote. What a tremendous change there would be if the Christian community became informed and involved!

As the power and potential of voting is explained to Christians, many wake up and act; others don't seem to respond at all! It is said that people fall into three categories: those who make things happen, those who sit and watch things happen, and those who don't even know that anything is happening until after it's all over. Too many Christians are in the third classification and even in the second—watching, but hesitant to get involved.

What Can You Do?

Many of us Americans have bought the line that there are two things that we must never talk about—religion and politics. But these are two areas that influence our lives and our futures most directly. Irene says, "We must begin to sense the urgency of Christ's commission and tell people about Jesus and His saving grace. And we need to talk about securing Christ-honoring leadership for our country. We ought to talk about the issues of politics."

Irene suggests specific ways you can make a difference:

1. Pray. That's the beginning point—on your knees every day before God who has the power to energize change that is needed. Pray daily for your country, your leadership, the future of your family.

2. Become informed. It is critical that you know what is happening! Read, read, read! Listen and learn. There are several fine publications emanating from Washinington, D.C. One of the best publications, *The Right Woman,* is designed to relay information concerning every piece of legislation that deals with women, children, and the family. It should be read by every Christian woman, and should be subscribed to by every Bible study group and every adult Sunday School class. Read the newspaper, even if the news is often negative. Read the news in light of Scripture, and evaluate it by the teachings of Jesus Christ. We must pray for great discernment!

3. Get involved. Be a part of what is going on in your town and your state. You may not have a tremendous influence on the national political scene, but you can make a substantial difference in your own community. In every community or neighborhood there are precincts where decisions are made about political candidates. It is on a precinct level that directions are set for the political party of your choice. It is in your locality that you can make a difference in government!

There is such a need for well-informed Christians with leadership ability, who are willing to run for public office. Imagine what a difference a Christian mayor or city councilman could make. Imagine what Christians on the school board might do, or Christian state legislators! Think of the difference it could make to have many Christians in the United States Senate and House of Representatives —people who would stand firm for godly principles.

Christians should be in every level of government. Frequently, while we have been sending our finest Christian young people to foreign mission fields as we have interpreted the Great Commission geographically, non-Christians have sent their finest into the mind-influencing areas of our country—into journalism, the media, seminaries, entertainment, education, religion, and into government and politics.

Christians need to become involved in drafting legislation. Consider phoning your legislator to suggest a piece of needed legislation.

But have a thoughtful presentation with carefully selected information on hand before you call.

Letters make a difference. The rule of thumb is that every letter reaching your legislator's desk represents 100 voters with similar views, who would have written had they been able to get around to it.

4. Register to vote.

5. Vote! You should vote in every single election that comes along, from the school board elections to the presidential election. Less than 10 percent of the people in this country vote in a school board election. In nonpresidential election years, less than half of our citizens turn out to vote for state legislators, or governors, or city councils. Imagine the impact if Christians always voted. That is where the action is—in the voting booth. This is not to say that there must be only one candidate for each office supported by the Christian community, but it is to say that each of us should find a candidate who upholds fine moral values and wants Jesus Christ exalted in our country. And then we should work for him or her. We are responsible for our elected officials. We *can* make a difference!

Linda Raney Wright and her husband reside in California. Serving on the staff of Campus Crusade for Christ, they frequently lecture on college campuses. Linda's articles have appeared in national magazines, and she has authored several books, including Raising Children *and* Success Helper.

21
Christian Perspective on Campus

From their home base in Southern California, Linda and Rusty Wright are on the go to college campuses across America. As staff members with Campus Crusade for Christ, they do extensive speaking and writing. Linda has several books to her credit, as well as numerous magazine articles. She was elected as one of the Outstanding Young Women of America in 1979.

Today, college campuses and classrooms boast of intellectual openness, yet the Wrights have found that the views presented are often imbalanced. Rusty was a student at Duke University when he first realized that the biblical perspective on life was rarely heard. He began a unique lecturing ministry to remedy this situation.

When Linda and Rusty were married in 1974, they committed themselves together to continue a full-time traveling and training schedule, bringing biblical light to the darkness of the college campus. Their strategy includes visiting a campus to train Campus

166

Crusade staff and students in a week-long seminar. During the seminar, the Wrights (and others) approach professors to ask for opportunities to lecture in classes.

Linda and Rusty have researched and prepared pertinent lectures representing the biblical viewpoint on a variety of subjects. Their list of topics includes: Atheism: A Realistic Option?, From Adam's Rib to Women's Lib, Business and Ethics, Evolution vs. Creation, and The Resurrection of Jesus Christ—Fact or Fiction?

Occasionally, a professor will object to the Christian viewpoint being expressed, using the law of separation of church and state as a point of reference. Linda says that this indicates a misunderstanding of the Supreme Court rulings:

"The constitutional viewpoint is that the state cannot *promote* a religious viewpoint, but there is no law which states that religion should not be discussed in schools at all. The Christian viewpoint should be brought in right along with the humanist perspective to give the students a proper balance so they can make their own choice."

The comment cards from the students, after Linda's and Rusty's presentations, have been a real source of encouragement to them. One said, ". . . very well presented as your ideas were not forced upon us. It is obvious you have done a lot of research and do not accept ideas without evidence."

Linda Wright has lectured at the University of Utah, Cornell University, and Arizona State, to name a few. She gave a commencement address at the University of California, Berkeley in 1971 and lectured at EXPLO 74 in Seoul, Korea.

Linda's Own Story

I became a Christian at age nine, and a Spirit-filled Christian my first year in college. During college years, I found that I had a lot of rerouting to do in my own personal life, in my character development, in my view of God, and in the matter of forming a good self-image.

Probably, the critical point in my Christian life came during an extended illness that put me flat on my back for three years. God used that time to strengthen my character. He slowed me down so I could think clearly about my life's direction. I am certain the spiritual growth I experienced then is a prime contributing factor to the ministry I have now.

When I began to seriously study the Bible, I got my own life together, and desired to help other people experience inner happiness.

My major in both high school and college was rhetoric, the art of speaking and writing correctly. In studying communication I began to notice that many ideas which are precious and meaningful to the Christian are not communicated well to the non-Christian. In fact, many Christians seem to be intellectual isolationists lacking interpersonal knowledge of the non-Christian and the world he lives in.

As I understood the Great Commission and the biblical perspective of why I was here—to share my faith and to make Christ known—I was motivated to reach the unreachable. As I studied some Christians, I began to realize that frequently it wasn't the Gospel message that many people rejected, but the approach used by the individual Christian. I felt that there was a way to understand the thinking of non-Christians, or confused Christians—emotionally, psychologically, intellectually, spiritually—so that I could communicate the Gospel to them.

Campus Ministry

This finally led to the adventure Rusty and I share—speaking and teaching in the university classroom. Our purpose is to present a well-rounded educational perspective of our subject. This means that we include various philosophical viewpoints. In studying different academic disciplines such as psychology, sociology, history, and philosophy, my husband and I have realized that there is a Christian perspective that is viable and important. The past five years of my life have been devoted to getting a grasp of these issues and making them intelligible to people of varying opinions and mind-sets. And it's exciting to train other Campus Crusade staff members to take advantage of lecture opportunities on secular campuses.

We also spend time teaching Christian students about the rights they have—they may present their own personal, Christian perspective during any class discussion of an issue. Students themselves can say almost anything in class related to the subject at hand, and some professors have even given students lecture time to present the Christian viewpoint!

Demoralization

In 1975, I began to be aware of an acceleration in the forces of evil. I found myself extremely bothered by the profanity, the shallowness, and the immoral sexual models evident in the movies and television. It seemed that our culture was steadily moving away from God.

As a communications major, I would sometimes watch the audience's reaction at a movie, or study the thinking of individuals watching TV. I could see that these people were being molded by a satanic force that pulled their thinking away from the Gospel and from a walk with God. I thought, *I have the Holy Spirit in me to convict me and to give me insight and this does provide me a certain amount of protection from what I am seeing. But those in the audience who, according to the biblical perspective, live in Satan's domain have no protection. They are being led astray! Christians with insight need to intervene and provide direction.*

I searched the Scriptures on this issue. I found that when Lot was in the wicked cities of Sodom and Gomorrah, he felt much the same way. Peter records that God destroyed Sodom and Gomorrah by fire, as an example for future ungodly people, but that God "rescued righteous Lot, oppressed by the sensual conduct of unprincipled men, (for by what he saw and heard, that righteous man, while living among them, felt his righteous soul tormented day after day with their lawless deeds)" (2 Peter 2:7-8 NASB).

I felt much like that. I began to pray fervently and persistently, asking the Lord to help our country and turn it around. I prayed for wisdom and answers to some questions that seemed to immobilize Christians and keep them from doing anything.

• As Christians should we become involved in social issues? Aren't we just supposed to preach the Gospel?

• If these are the end times, aren't things *supposed* to get bad before the Lord comes back? If so, then what Christians do won't make any difference, will it?

• As a Christian, do I have a right to impose my values on others?

• Does my Christianity affect America? Or does America affect my Christianity?

I find that most Christians feel confused about civil rights, censorship, the First Amendment, and other issues related to government. You can tell them they ought to be doing something, but they have mental blocks.

Prime Concerns

At present my biggest concern is in the area of social issues. I am concerned about the toleration of homosexuality in our country, for I believe that the open practice of homosexuality is a major step downward for a nation. Christians are confused on this issue. Some Christians feel guilty if they take a strong stand against the sin of homosexuality, since they know they should love the sinner and communicate the grace of God to him.

I am concerned that the media are not being used to influence people positively in shaping character or even in the building of basic human principles. Rather they are being used in a destructive process to lead people away from God.

I am concerned about abortion, the conscienceless taking of human lives.

I am concerned about the increase in pornography—about escalating crime, about schools that seem unable to teach basic subjects adequately or to build character. A great many specific issues are constantly on my mind, and many Christians are similarly burdened.

I am working on a book to help Christians better understand some of these issues and troublesome questions. It will include "how tos" for individual homemakers and church or community small groups.

Motion Pictures

I have campaigned against objectionable movies in my community— I have written letters; I have talked to store managers, movie theater owners, and people who run shopping malls. I have tried to inspire Christians not to get discouraged in the fight.

There are many steps you as a Christian can take to influence the motion picture industry. You can refuse to attend "questionable" movies. You can call or visit the theater to register concern over objectionable movies being shown in your neighborhood, with a follow-up letter to the theater and to the film producer.

You can write a *general letter to motion picture personnel,* similar to the following sample.

Dear Sirs:

I am very concerned about the moral and spiritual development of our country. In light of this, I feel that the motion picture industry should keep the caliber of its films at a level that will promote such things as decency, the worth of the individual, faith, hope, hard work, and responsibility.

I urge that actors and actresses and all other members of the industry take a stand against allowing such destructive subject matter as demonology, homosexuality, extra-marital affairs, blasphemy to God and Christ, erosion of spiritual and religious principles, the occult, astrology, and the like to be used in films.

I further urge that the ratings on movies be more strict. Minors should be excluded from movies with a parental guidance rating. These movies now include such things as sex orgies, massive violence, filthy language, and homosexual liaisons. However, it is my feeling that this material is also destructive to adults in our society and eventually to all of us.

As a Christian, my concern is for the total fulfillment of every individual. It is in this regard that I ask you to promote things that will bring integrity and respect back to the people of our nation.

Thank you if this is your choice. Also, thank you for future choices of a positive nature.

Sincerely,

(your signature)

Send xeroxed copies of your letter to local theaters, local cable TV stations, major motion picture companies and to:

1. President
   Screen Actors' Guild
   7750 Sunset Boulevard
   Los Angeles, CA 90046
2. Motion Picture Association of America
   8480 Beverly Boulevard
   Los Angeles, CA 90048
   (This is where pictures are rated.)

TV

As Christians we must also take note of what is happening to TV. Foul language, lusty bed scenes, blatant attacks on God and religion, the stripping of values, rampant violence, and the self-centered philosophy of living based on relative standards can be found on any public station, including educational TV.

Egotistical, anti-God individuals are manipulating the public media. We need to support efforts to clean up TV programming.

We who are the light of the world can see that negative aspects of TV programming are discontinued, and we can be instrumental in bringing the Christian perspective to the attention of the world via TV.

You can take action by writing a *general letter to television sponsors and the three major networks* asking for improved programming. A sample letter follows which could be adapted and put in your own words. Send copies to local stations and television stars.

Dear Sirs:

I am writing as an American citizen to voice my concern over the recent moral and spiritual decay as presented in the media. The TV media present a persuasive message.

Recently they have aired material of a questionable nature: extreme violence, sex scenes, foul language. They have also undermined moral and spiritual values on many levels.

As one of your viewers, may I urge you not only to delete some of the shallow, self-centered programming which is currently being shown, but urge you to present materials that will inspire the American people: themes of faith, decency, hard work, and respectability.

I urge you not to be among those who are bringing the occult, witchcraft, astrology and satanism into our culture. I am also opposed to the positive treatment of homosexuality. Most of all, I hope you will include more Christian programming which will help people know about our wonderful Lord and how they can know Him personally.

Thank you for considering my point of view.

Sincerely,

(your signature)

P.S. Could you let me know your network's future plans concerning this?

NATIONAL NETWORK ADDRESSES

ABC, 1330 Avenue of the Americas, New York, New York 10019 Phone: (212) 887-7777

CBS, 51 West 52nd Street, New York, New York 10019 Phone: (212) 975-4321

NBC, 30 Rockefeller Plaza, New York, New York 10020 Phone: (212) 664-4444

You can also call local stations immediately if you view a TV show containing questionable subject matter. Your complaint to the local sponsor is most important. To obtain addresses of TV sponsors write "Directory of Advertising Products and Programs by TV Sponsors" to Television Product Cross-Reference Directory, Everglades Publishing Company, Everglades, Florida 53929.

Linda gives these suggestions for writing a *specific complaint letter:*

1. Do not preach. Present your opinion.
2. The tone should register concern rather than anger.
3. Express your *own* position. Don't act as if you are writing for 10 people you know. The media are wise to this and will count your letter as one opinion. (You could take a vote of an organization and write that you are representing 44 women from the John Adams Elementary School PTA, who voted on February 1, 1976 about this matter. This is valid. A petition is also valid.)
4. Suggest an alternative if possible.
5. There are two basic arguments. The first is economic. Convince those involved that they are losing viewers, hence money, by their actions. The second is community or national integrity. Point out the moral responsibility they have to the people of this nation.
6. Give the *specifics* of what you saw. Some sponsors aren't aware of what they are sponsoring.
7. Let sponsors know you will not buy their products. Then follow-through with your commitment.
8. Express appreciation for the good TV programming.
9. For educational TV, write whoever gives a grant. At the end of the show the announcer will say, "This program is made possible by a grant from: Exxon, etc."
10. Ask for a response.

As few as 25 phone calls or 5 letters can make a positive difference. Yours could be the one!

Encouraging Possibilities

As I have become increasingly involved during these past six years, I have been somewhat encouraged. I see the possibility for Christians to mobilize and bring many people to Christ. Bit by bit we are gaining strength. However, it is a long, hard fight and demands righteousness in our lives, as well as courage and active participation in confronting evil.

Martha Rountree is a lecturer, journalist, radio and television personality, and a political analyst of national and world affairs. She received the George Foster Peabody Award, and is two-time recipient of the Academy of Radio and Television Arts And Sciences Award. Martha founded Leadership Foundation, Inc., based in Washington, D.C.

22
Foundation for Freedom

If you are old enough to remember the early years of "Meet the Press" on television, you may also remember seeing an attractive moderator with an engaging southern accent. Martha Rountree was creator and co-producer of this and several other award-winning TV programs. She has also lectured, and worked in radio and journalism. She was named "Woman of the Year" by the Business and Professional Woman in Chicago and St. Louis and by the Associated Press editors, and has been featured in such periodicals as *Time* and *Reader's Digest.*

She is an unforgettable woman with great persistence and self-discipline. These qualities have played a significant part in her many accomplishments, which include the founding of Leadership Founddation, Inc.

Miss Rountree is a member of the Washington Press Club. She has served on the Board of Governors of the Women's National Republic Club since 1960. She also serves on the Board of the Lincoln Law

Center, Board of Directors for American Cause, and several other influential boards.

She is a member of the National Presbyterian Church. As you read her story, you will sense her heart's desire that our beloved country would return to God-honoring, God-fearing moral principles.

I was fascinated as Miss Rountree described her Washington apartment to me, with its dozens of file drawers bulging with documented information about her concerns for our country, including her work to see voluntary prayer put back in our schools. How I admire her convincing commitment!

Martha Tells Her Story

So many times we hear people tell us that when they were facing death, all the events of their past came flooding back. This was not my experience when I suffered a heart attack in 1968. My first reaction was one of disbelief. It was so unexpected. There was no warning. It was only after I passed the crisis, was removed from intensive care, and spent weeks in a sunshiny hospital room, that details of my life passed through my mind.

The thoughts began with my wonderful, beautiful, and gallant mother who believed her daughter to be the most talented person in the world. She felt that I could achieve anything. From the time I was a child, she made me feel very special—that God had great plans for me, that I had talents which must not be squandered.

I remembered, also, my grandmother who scolded me for growing cross with a playmate who had been unkind. Patiently, she explained that I should feel sorry for someone who was unfair, that I could not retaliate. When I got older, I asked her what she meant. Why couldn't I fight back when I was wronged? Why was I supposed to be different? She gave me this answer: "Because you are a child of God and He expects you to set an example. No one is cruel or hateful on purpose. You must act better and set a good example for others."

Growing Up in the Depression

In my growing-up years, much was expected of me and my four brothers and sisters. My father had died early in the 1930s. My mother, still very young, set about to weather the rough years in the South when the depression had reduced almost everyone to the same economic level. My mother set an example of strength for us, and she would not accept anything but the best efforts from her children. We were a very close family. All of us worked, earned our way through school, and helped with household chores. We contributed from our limited resources to charities in the community, went to Sunday School and church, and shared with our friends. Not once did our mother seem to falter, shed a tear before us, or indicate any doubt that all would be well and that each of us would be achievers. Disappointing her was out of the question.

Later, I went to New York to try out those talents Mother had hypnotized me into believing I had. It was ironic that when my first big break came, the very day my first network program made its debut, Mother—just 46—learned she had cancer. Throughout the next few years, as I struggled up the ladder, Mother was dying by the day.

She did have the satisfaction of knowing that all of her children fulfilled their promise. One of my sisters became well-known in the fashion world; a brother was a successful design engineer; the youngest son in our family produced his first Broadway play at age 17. He was drafted the next year and injured in the Korean War. He has spent the remaining years in a hospital. Another sister chose to stay in the South, accomplished in her role as mother and homemaker.

Whatever we have done, it has been possible because we had a great and courageous mother who gave us faith and hope, who set high moral standards and values for us, and who made us feel that everything was possible with God's help.

Citizenship Was Encouraged

Of course, there were others who helped to shape my character and my future. There was the wonderful eighth-grade American history teacher who made me understand the meaning of responsible citizenship. Miss Ida M. Price taught in a Philadelphia school where I spent one year. On Saturdays Miss Price took me to see places associated with the birth and development of our country— Independence Hall, the home of Betsy Ross, and Valley Forge Park where we went picnicking and I listened as she made history come alive. She encouraged me to enter an essay contest entitled "How to Be a Loyal American." I won second prize. My offering was a little too brief to qualify for first prize (an error I have not repeated in any of my adult ventures).

In addition to using her own time to go over my essay with a fine-tooth comb—discussing the content, inspiring me to do several rewrites, and, yes, even correcting the grammar—Miss Price took the opportunity to instill gratitude for the privilege of being an American. She spelled out the deprivation and pain experienced by so many others around the world. She brought home to me the exciting fact that every boy and girl in the United States can grow up to be whatever he or she wishes. The only requirement is the choice of the right field—one that fits a young person's talents—and the willingness to work.

There also was Harry R. Trusler, dean of the law school at the University of Florida. I was five when the Truslers, who had a daughter near my age, moved several doors from my grandparents' home. I loved to read and, seeing this, Dean Trusler made available his large collection of law books—inspiring in me as I grew older, a serious interest and respect for our legal system. But he gave me even more. I cherish and am guided by a bit of poetry he wrote for me when I was six or seven:

Good Morning, Martha, do get up! Put on your cap and run.
The road is not on any map. It fades out in the sun.

At home, an aunt used to remind us about our family tree, remarking that the ability to deal properly with life depends on the quality of one's background. But Mother would say, "It's the other way around. It's not who you are but *what* you are." She would laughingly say, "People are like potatoes. The best part of them seems to be underground." She insisted that "where you come from is not nearly so important as where you are going."

How much the things we learn as children influence our later lives! Throughout the years, there were a number of homilies to guide us. When a family member got upset about something, he was reminded that "nothing is ever eaten as hot as it is cooked." We grew up with "Better late than never," and "Do unto others as you would have them do unto you." Older people always seemed to have an easily understandable and tested bit of philosophy to illustrate a point.

Young People Are Impressionable

I had a lot of time to think during the long months of convalescence after that 1968 heart attack. I acknowledged how good life had been to me, and recognized the importance of being part of a close family and growing up loved, encouraged to pursue whatever talents I had. I realized what it means for a young person to have someone older single him out and make him feel important. Moreover, I came to see that we adults often do not know what an important part we may be playing in a young person's life. Little acts of kindness and taking the time to pay attention can have significant meaning in later years.

Today, life has become very impersonal. People living next door to each other may never become acquainted. Millions of youngsters do not know what it is to go home after school and find their mothers waiting for them, because so many women must work. A schoolteacher friend of mine, commenting on today's juvenile crime, refers to those children who stumble along the way as "latch key kids." They carry a house key, and are on their own long before they have learned how to handle such independence.

Our future leaders will have to be chosen from today's youth. America can grow no bigger, no better, and no stronger than our young people. But, we have a great problem to deal with today: Juvenile crime accounts for over 50 percent of serious crimes—rape, murder, assault, larceny, theft, arson, drug addiction and drug pushing, vandalism, and so on. How did our children get into this situation? The community, the home, and the church have failed.

I have traveled across the nation, speaking in 48 states over the past nine years. Everywhere I have found concerned parents and citizens. I have found few people who were not troubled for our country, and most especially for our youth.

Now, why can't the women of America come together and do something to turn the tide? We know that real concern exists. We know that our people do not intentionally turn their backs on our young citizens. Let's examine the problem a little closer.

Too Big Too Fast?

As I remember my childhood and that of my peers, I know we were important to members of the community. We were loved and valued by our teachers, the shopkeepers, and our neighbors. I have come to the conclusion that somewhere along the line, America started changing.

Perhaps it was because we had gotten too big too fast, or perhaps, after World War II, people couldn't stand prosperity, couldn't accept the responsibilities that went along with success. An affluent society gave young people too many material things and perhaps this indulgence replaced the appearance of loving and caring. Perhaps too adults lost sight of the need to set an example for the youth of our country. In the doing, we may have created an impersonal, selfish, and apathetic approach to life—one that has replaced old-fashioned standards, traditions, incentives, and responsibilities.

Leadership Foundation, Inc.

I was personally encouraged to do something back in 1964 when I received a call from a wonderful lady, Mrs. Catharine Sanford in Flint, Michigan. She said, "Martha, our country is in trouble and we need leadership. You are the one to do something about it."

Unbelievable as it sounds, three other ladies from three different states called me within a few weeks' time to say almost the same thing. "We need leadership, and we want to work with you."

As a result, a group of concerned friends joined with me in starting Leadership Foundation, Inc. This is an umbrella organization to bring concerned women in America together in a concerted, grass-roots effort to restore moral and spiritual values to our country. At the same time, the Foundation determined to develop an information center to research and disseminate facts to the women of America regarding key legislative issues.

Initially, we were a bit unsure of ourselves and uncertain about how to achieve such worthy goals. We started a few chapters in five or six states, and I did what I could. However, at that time I had a career to worry about. It was not until I suffered the heart attack in 1968 that it occurred to me I might have been singled out for a very special job. I felt guilty because the Foundation had not accomplished much. I was determined that if the Lord spared my life, I would enthusiastically try to live up to the expectations of those who had reached out to me.

War on Pornography

In 1970 I began to accept every speaking invitation that would take me into the grass roots to meet and talk with concerned women. The Foundation took shape and our accomplishments began to mount. One of our first projects was a campaign to stop the spread of pornography through the mail. In 1970 smut mail was a billion dollar business in the United States. Even children were receiving it.

In 1972 Senator Barry Goldwater of Arizona had been successful in getting an amendment to the postal bill through Congress, which made it possible to deal with this issue. The legislative solution was simple: If you did not want to receive sexually oriented materials in the mail, all you had to do was to go to the post office and fill out a form. If, after 30 days you still received such materials in the mail and you reported it to the postmaster, those responsible would be in violation of the law and subject to a fine, imprisonment, or both.

But, in time, it became obvious that the forms were a problem. They were tedious and difficult to handle. Moreover, it was not easy for women with young children to stand in line to get information and forms to complete. More importantly, few people seemed aware of the Goldwater legislation. Finally, the *New York Times* printed a story stating that so few forms had been processed, it would seem only Senator Goldwater was concerned over smut mail.

Leadership Foundation decided to make special forms available to its members. We explained the legislation and its intent to our members. As a result of the Foundation's work, there were almost 100 indictments and many convictions against those peddling sexually oriented materials through the mails. The Foundation was commended by Senator Goldwater and the Department of Justice. *Reader's Digest* printed an article which credited Leadership Foundation for its work in helping to eliminate sexually oriented materials from the United States mails.

Community Standards' Committees

A 1973 Supreme Court decision cleared the way for towns, cities, and states to set their own moral standards, giving citizens the right to pass local laws or ordinances to uphold the moral standards in their own communities. Based on that Supreme Court decision, Leadership Foundation developed a citizen's action program which we call Community Standards' Committees.

The first Community Standards' Committee was established in Portsmouth, Virginia. It has been so successful in dealing with the moral problems in that area, we have taken our guidelines from its history.

Our goal today is to help establish a Community Standards' Committee in every town and city in America. We only have to look at the Portsmouth, Virginia success to realize what can be done if enough citizens come together to deal with their problems. Through these committees, citizens get to know each other; people from across town suddenly find the folks on the other side sharing mutual concerns. A Community Standards' Committee works to eliminate apathy and to stimulate interest among neighbors and members of the community. The result is that citizens become involved.

Voluntary Prayer in Schools

We made another big push at this time for restoring voluntary prayer in our schools. Until 1962 school children in many states assembled for a morning prayer, the Pledge of Allegiance to the Flag, and often a patriotic song. Today these are things of the past. Prayer has been banned; the Pledge of Allegiance has been eliminated in many schools. Even Christmas pageants, dramas, and carols are forbidden, as are invocations and benedictions at special ceremonies.

Because of this trend, we are losing effective sources of moral and ethical conditioning for our young people. Crime among school-age juveniles has increased dramatically. Vandalism in schools, churches, and against private property is rampant. A drug culture threatens to dominate our society. Juvenile theft is taken for granted. Juvenile arson, murder, muggings, and rape are high on the national crime list.

It is significant to note that this moral decline among the youth of America has taken place during the 17 years since prayer was first taken out of the schools. What kind of leaders can we expect in future years?

How could we have let this happen and what can we do about it? The obvious solution is for voters to demand congressional action. Congress could have remedied this situation long ago if people had called for action in a united, concerted drive.

In April 1979 legislation to restore voluntary prayer in the schools was passed in the United States Senate by a vote 51 to 40. The bill, introduced by Senator Jesse Helms of North Carolina, limits the jurisdiction of the federal courts and the Supreme Court in the area of school prayer. This legislation does not tamper with the Constitution in any way. On the contrary, it invokes the Constitution, following to the letter the guarantees it sets forth.

Section 2, Article III states in clear and precise language that the appellate jurisdiction of the Court is subject to "such exceptions and under such regulations, as the Congress shall make."

"Fortunately," says Senator Helms, "The Constitution provides this alternative under the system of checks and balances. In anticipation of judicial usurpation of power, the framers of our Constitution wisely gave Congress the authority, by a simple majority of both houses, to check the Supreme Court through regulation of its appellate jurisdiction. This is what this bill to restore freedom of prayer in the public schools will accomplish."

Several points are noteworthy. The bill (S. 450), when enacted into law, will only provide the right to pray in school. It will not force anyone to participate in school prayer against his wishes. Also, it does not presume to specify any particular or special prayers. It only restores an important Constitutional right to communities, and states the Constitutional right of freedom of religion. Although the Supreme Court and the federal courts are barred from interfering, local and state courts would have the right to arbitrate any problems that might arise. In short, states' rights and constitutional rights would be restored with the passage of the Helms legislation.

For the first time in almost 18 years, prayer legislation has been voted out of the Senate. If 218 members of the House of Representatives vote for the bill in 1980, prayer in the schools will become a reality before the 1980 elections.

This is dependent upon the will of the voters, particularly in contacting members of the House of Representatives who are seeking reelection in November 1980. If the voters in each congressional district make their voices heard and make their feelings known to their congressmen, there is no doubt that we can succeed in returning prayer to our schools. National polls have shown that well over 85 percent of the public has expressed itself as wanting voluntary prayer for our children. Now is the time for that 85 percent to take a stand.

The Voters' Choice

At Leadership Foundation, we believe that there is no problem in our nation that cannot be solved if we, as the voters, take advantage of the opportunity to speak out. If we elect responsible men and women to office, we will have responsible government. Through the exercise of our vote, we can determine our way of life. Through default, we can lose our freedoms.

It has been said that in the seeds of democracy are also sown the seeds of destruction. Through apathy or lack of information, we can destroy the essential goodness of our country. Through responsible use of our rights of citizenship, we can reaffirm the principles upon which this nation was founded. As the Pledge of Allegiance reminds us, God must be a part of all processes in which we engage. A nation that is not under God is a nation without God.

Trudy Camping, fourth-term Arizona state senator, is the mother of six children and grandmother to nine. She was "First Runner-Up, Arizona Mother of the Year" in 1978. Trudy was twice voted "Outstanding State Legislator," and has authored periodical and encyclopedia articles relating to the ERA.

23
Grandma Is a Senator

Should *Christians* be in politics? Should Christian *women* be in politics?

Trudy Camping maintains that an elected position in state or federal government certainly is not for everyone, but it *is* for her! Trudy Camping has found her niche—her place to help "build the wall"—and she works very hard as fourth-term senator in the Arizona State Legislature.

Her particular district has only 40 percent registered Republicans, so Trudy's win in 1970—and her reelection every two years since—are ample evidence of God's design for her life.

Trudy was born of Dutch parents in the farming community of Edgerton, Minnesota during the Roaring Twenties. A strong Christian home provided a sure foundation, and a love for God with a disciplined study of the Word was built into her life.

Question: Can a girl from a little farming town in the Midwest find happiness as the wife of a western newspaper photographer?

Answer: Yes! Ralph Camping made Trudy his bride in 1944, in

183

Denver, Colorado. They moved to Phoenix in 1947, and Ralph became the photographer for the *Arizona Republic*. They had been married 20 years when Ralph died in 1964.

Trudy is the mother of six children—four sons and two daughters. Only one child is still at home with her, but Trudy is frequently visited by her nine grandchildren. In 1978, Trudy was first runner-up for the title of "Arizona Mother of the Year"!

Picking Up the Pieces

The early days of widowhood were traumatic and difficult for Trudy, but God faithfully assured and reassured her at that time. As she felt His peace and stability, she began to rebuild her life.

Trudy enrolled in Phoenix Junior College for a two-year business and secretarial course. This qualification opened the door to a position as secretary to the dean of women at North High School in Phoenix for several years.

She continued lay service in her Christian Reformed Church, and her work on the Phoenix Christian Grade School Board was fulfilling and challenging. But in 1970 the greatest challenge of her life came her way!

Senate Seat

As a registered Republican, with no background in politics or party involvement, Trudy was asked to run for the state senate seat in District 25. The incumbent Republican had sponsored and voted for many bills which had embarrassed the members of his party; consequently the citizens were not pleased with his voting record and wanted a change.

Through an important chain of events, Trudy became convinced it was within God's plan and providence that she should run against the incumbent senator. She won in the primary and then campaigned against a former legislator in the general election. In 1971 she took the senate seat and began a new career!

ERA

Trudy has been instrumental in maintaining Arizona as one of the states that has so far refused to ratify the Equal Rights Amendment.

Trudy is opposed to the ERA, first, because it is unnecessary. Second, she feels that the imprecise language will produce undesirable interpretations in the courts. Third, she feels the states will be rendered meaningless, because power will be transferred from the states to the federal government.

Senator Camping says that many qualifying amendments to the ERA text were offered and defeated in Congress before it was submitted for the states' ratification. "There is no possible doubt that Congress intended ERA to be total and absolute; to nullify all existing superior rights of women in regard to family, the military, manual labor, crimes, and privacy" (*The Christian Reader,* January 1979).

Mrs. Camping is unable to support such problematic legislation. Unlike a law, a ratified constitutional amendment is "set in cement." It can only be reversed by going through the entire amending process again.

Trudy Camping is concerned for the welfare of women, and cites Arizona as an example of the progress in women's rights, without ratification of the proposed amendment, and without a state ERA. According to Trudy: "Women in Arizona are in every area of government, business, and education. These women have attained their positions, not because they are women, but because they are qualified and have worked for them. There are 4 women senators and 13 representatives serving in the Arizona legislature. Out of the 17 only 4 are pro-ERA. Those who are opposed see it as being harmful to the traditional family and as a complete takeover of states' rights by the federal government."

Focus on Family

Trudy is most concerned about the family unit, and related issues of children's rights, pornography, quality public education, and threats to Christian school systems. She is concerned about trends in education toward behavior modification and value clarification, which are sowing the seeds of anarchy.

Senator Camping takes action in her sphere of influence. She speaks and appears on radio and TV, writes for publications, and debates with those holding pro-ERA, pro-IYC, and pro-pornography positions.

She has served on the Arizona Home and Family Committee, the Arizona Obscenity Task Force, Citizens for Decency through Law, and other committees.

"I have sponsored several bills which are now in our statutes on pornography. First, we defined what obscenity was and second, passed the public nuisance law which allows a community to rid itself of adult bookstores and theatres if it wishes. I also led a successful fight against the nomination of a lawyer, who has defended pornography for 20 years, to be a member of the Selection Committee for Judges.

"I have seen more Constitutional rights being taken away by government and bureaucratic agencies. My involvement has helped to preserve freedom of religion and to protect our Christian schools.

"I believe God has used me in a significant way in government. Looking back, I can see His hand in my being there when He took control of matters. Sometimes my vote has made a difference for Arizona. Other times God has used my one vote to influence legislation that has affected the whole United States."

Sarah Maddox is the wife of a business-man and mother of two teenagers. A former English teacher, she has served as president of the Baptist Women. Sarah is active in the Memphis chapter of Leadership Foundation, and has directed a Christian Women's Concerns Conference.

24
A Flair for Priorities

"I truly believe that one person can do something—through the strength of the One who lives within us—Jesus Christ, our Lord!" This has been the philosophy of Sarah Odle Maddox since the early 1970s when she began to live out the principles of that little verse which states: "I am only one, but I am one. I cannot do everything, but I can do something. And by God's grace, that thing I will do."

Somewhere it seems that Christians have gotten the idea that one person cannot do any good in fighting the evils in our society. For years many believers have felt that combating moral pollution was someone else's responsibility. But women like Sarah have "stood in the gap," seeking to motivate and inspire Christian women to get involved.

"When I first started fighting against violence and explicit sex on television, many people (including some Christians), said to me, 'Oh, just turn off the television set. Don't let your children watch it.' I questioned them about the thousands of children in our city whose parents were not turning off the TV. Did I not have a responsibility to them as well? That was in the early 70s. Today, in 1980, people

187

everywhere are 'up in arms' saying, 'Let's do something about television!' I believe that if we would have taken action sooner in this area, much good could have been accomplished.

"My involvement in combating moral pollution," Sarah relates, "has represented a sometimes unpopular position. But Jesus set the example for us—His was a lonely road. When I have needed assistance in this battle, God has always sent His warriors. And I believe our labors have been worthwhile—truly worth the effort. When I see what has happened in Arkansas, and know that if I had not said or done anything, the results would have been quite different, I feel truly rewarded."

Godly Heritage

Sarah Maddox's grandfather, L.R. Riley, was a Baptist minister. Her father, Joe T. Odle, is a Baptist minister, and she and her husband Roland are deeply involved in the ministry of Bellevue Baptist Church in Memphis, Tennessee. Her active participation ranges from teaching a Sunday School class of college and career women to preparing for a Foreign Missions Week of Prayer or accompanying a children's choir.

Sarah's minister father was the editor of a Southern Baptist newspaper until his retirement just a few years ago. "I am grateful to God for the heritage of dynamic service and love for Jesus Christ exemplified in my home by my father and mother."

Southern Baptist blood is surely in her veins. With her business-man husband and her two teenage children, their home in Memphis, Tennessee is a powerhouse of creative, purposeful activity. God's purpose and plan for their lives is central and each family member feels a strong commitment to live as God's person.

Mississippi College (Baptist), just five miles from the state capital of Jackson, became Sarah's alma mater. Her evident gifts of leadership and interest in government were awakened under the shadow of the state capitol, for she was elected Miss Mississippi College, and served as president of the Women's Student Government. She graduated with honors, having a major in sociology, and minors in music, English, and secondary education.

Sarah followed this preparation with a move to Memphis to teach junior high English. Here Roland Maddox met Sarah and married her. Bellevue Baptist Church became their church home and the hub of their service to the Lord.

Music has played an important part in Sarah's life. She has taught piano and she has been pianist for the Bible Study Fellowship and numerous other organizations. She has also served as leader, chairman, or president of various organizations in Memphis.

God's New Direction

Seven years ago Sarah sensed God's special call to her, and with resolve she appropriated these words: "Remember the Lord, who is great and awesome, and fight for your brothers, your sons and your daughters, your wives and your homes" (Neh. 4:14b, NIV).

Sarah, herself, was contented with her life. "For me, it was a joy to be a *woman*—a female created to have fellowship with God and to become *conformed to the image of His Son*. It was a privilege to be an *American* woman with more luxuries, more modern conveniences and more freedoms than women anywhere else in the world."

But looking around her, Sarah noticed a movement afoot which was causing many American women to rethink their positions, their purposes, and priorities. She saw women surfacing everywhere, demanding their rights and freedoms.

Perhaps it was the publication of *The Feminine Mystique* by Betty Friedan that had triggered consciouness-raising meetings and widespread dissatisfaction among women concerning their lot in life, their jobs, and their profession of homemaking. Women were being told that they had been "dealt a terrible blow," that females were "handicapped." Had someone pushed a panic button to cause such turmoil and chaos in the world of women?

"Lord, what would You have me to do?" became Sarah's prayer. And God was swift to answer. Sharing the love of Christ had always been a top priority for Sarah, and the Lord clearly opened a new channel for her to express His love.

God's direction was evident as Sarah attended a meeting where Martha Rountree, founder of "Meet the Press" news program on radio and television, was speaking. The other speaker was Vonette Bright, wife of the director of Campus Crusade for Christ. Their subject was "Moral Pollution." Mrs. Rountree told about founding a group in Washington called Leadership Foundation, dedicated to fighting moral pollution in our country. Sarah recalls, "The organization was soon to have a national convention in Washington at the same time my husband and I were to be there for a business convention. God was igniting a desire in my heart to learn and to become involved in these concerns. What Martha and Vonette said that day deeply stirred my heart!

"I prayed for several days for God's direction, and I earnestly desired His will about my involvement. Kneeling before God, my Bible open, my eyes fell on Nehemiah 4:14 (NASB)—'Remember the Lord . . . fight . . . for your houses,' and I sensed God's leadership in this direction."

While attending the Leadership Foundation convention, Sarah had heard many disturbing things—warnings about the effect of TV violence on children's minds and behavior, the growing drug problem, changes in school textbooks from old-fashioned character building to absence of moral values, and debates on the proposed Equal Rights Amendment.

Sarah was jolted into action. She felt inadequate in her understanding of the issues, but she returned home determined to learn all she could about the ERA and each of the other concerns to which she had been exposed.

A chapter of Leadership Foundation was formed in Memphis and Sarah became actively involved in monitoring TV programs, contacting sponsors, informing parents and civic groups of the danger to children inherent in large doses of TV violence and explicit sex. But it was the women's liberation movement, and its growing influence in matters that affect all of us, that called forth her most lasting response!

What about Women?

First, Sarah made an intense study of the women's liberation movement. It was obvious to her that not everything about this movement had been detrimental to society. It had called attention to the discrimination against women down through history, and had promoted such legislation as the Equal Employment Opportunity Act, the Equal Pay Act, and legislation for equal credit privileges and educational opportunities.

But as Sarah examined the goals and philosophies of the feminist leaders, she decided that the negative outweighed the positive! One example of the negative was the desire of many feminists for a unisex society—with calls for a change ranging from "no more pink or blue baby blankets" to rewording the Bible for "total sexual equality."

Anna Stassiropolis in her book, *The Female Woman,* explained that some feminists believe all differences in men and women (except in the reproductive systems) to be harmful, inflicted on women by men as a result of social conditioning. These feminists believe we can condition people away from these stereotypes to produce a gender-free society.

Sarah believes that the concept of *unisex* opposes God's plan. "God created us male and female. If a woman rebels against her femininity, she is rebelling against God. Christian women have been used mightily by God through the centuries from Esther and Lydia in the Bible times to modern-day Ann Judson, Annie Armstrong, and Corrie ten Boom. I believe God used them for particular purposes *because* they were women, *not in spite of the fact.*"

Sarah has shared the results of her research and Bible study with women's groups in many corners of the middle South in Southern Baptist and other evangelical churches, as well as with civic organizations. She stresses that it is our particular feminine characteristics that have made us suited for special tasks and that we will be used by God, not because we demand the right to be just like the men, but because we are submissive to God's will.

ERA
Most feminists are committed to the passage of the ERA, believing that through it equality in legal treatment of the sexes will become a reality. Sarah disagrees. "No amendment can bring an end to discrimination," she says. But her ideas about the ERA extend further. As a result of her many years of study, she believes that the amendment is unrealistic and unnecessary. "In Tennessee we got busy and worked to rescind the ERA. We are not certain if the rescission will hold up in the final analysis, but our voices have been heard. The will of the majority has been made known!"

Sarah learned early about being properly equipped for spiritual warfare. "When I came home from the Leadership Foundation Convention in Washington, a friend called and asked me to testify before some legislators at a local town meeting. I can remember how inadequate I felt to speak before this group. My friend gave me a prepared statement to read, but the entire time I was fearful that I would be asked a question I could not answer. I determined then that before I would speak on a subject, I would learn everything I could about the issues and carefully document all specific information. I made a commitment to speak only when and where the Lord directed me. I believe our Lord expects us to represent Him well and to speak boldly and confidently in the power of His name. We are engaged in a spiritual battle. Not only must we know our subjects, but we must put on our spiritual armor before we go out into the world. When we step into the battle fully armed, great victories can be won!

"Twice I have had the opportunity to take part in local TV talk shows. A minister's wife and I were scheduled on a morning when a nationally known entertainer was to be the featured guest. The well-known guest never made it to the station and practically the entire hour was given to us to speak against the ERA."

Phyllis Schlafly asked Sarah to go to Florida to speak against the proposed 27th amendment. Because she was unable at that time to go, she called two of her friends in Florida, urging them to get to work. And they did! To back up their efforts, she wrote to many Southern Baptist pastors in that state, giving her reasons for being against the amendment. She urged them to vote against the ERA and to use their influence against it. She gathered support in Missouri, Illinois, and North Carolina also.

Sarah could not keep silent. She expressed her views and influenced others to speak out, to write letters, and to make telephone calls. One of her special gifts is to motivate others. (Just talk to some of her friends who have addressed many letters!)

And Mrs. Maddox's commitment broadened. She says, "The more concerned I became about the ERA and its effects on our country, the more concerned I became about the goals and philosophies of those leading the women's liberation movement. So many good women had gotten caught up in the movement, believing it to be simply a drive for equal pay for equal work. The International Women's Year meetings exposed some of the dangerous and unbiblical goals of the radical feminists. I had planned to attend the Tennessee IWY, but had a conflict with family vacation plans. When a mother is faced with the choice of her desires and those of her family, her family must come first."

My Neighbors in Arkansas

"Since I could not attend our state IWY, I urged Marilyn Simmons, a friend in Arkansas, to attend the Arkansas IWY. She was so disturbed about the events of that meeting, she later paid her own way to Washington to testify at Senator Jesse Helms' ad hoc hearings.

"You can motivate your friends into action too! If you never testify at hearings or appear on television shows, you can share your convictions. One night we had dinner with our friends in Arkansas, along with their pastor and his wife. In our dinner conversation, I told them about our getting the ERA rescinded in Tennessee. Then I said, 'You all really need to do something in Arkansas!' "

The pastor and his wife readily admitted that they did not know enough to speak either for or against the amendment. They wanted to know more. A few days later Sarah was invited to come back to Little Rock to speak to a group of concerned Christian women, a group which included the pastor's wife. This important trip led to an opportunity for Sarah to speak at a breakfast for all the Arkansas legislators and also to a meeting of pastors and wives and other Christian leaders. At this second event, Sarah turned over the ball to the Arkansans, for them to carry on the work there.

And how they did! A group was formed which eventually came to be called *Flag,* representing family, life, America, God. Marilyn Simmons became its director. This group has done a phenomenal job in mobilizing into action the pro-family people of Arkansas. The pastor and his wife have boldly taken a stand against moral pollution and have had great influence among Baptists in Arkansas and elsewhere.

Sarah says, "I get excited every time I think about it, because it took so little of my effort. All it took was my being enthusiastic about what *we* were doing and my urging *them to get involved.* There isn't a woman in America who can't participate with enthusiasm and then encourage someone else to get involved—to pray earnestly and then to act in the power of the Holy Spirit."

IWY

In the fall of 1977, Sarah and those who shared her concerns accepted a new challenge—to inform women of the Middle South about the IWY and women's lib. Sarah says, "I really felt led of the Holy Spirit to hold a rally at our church. The national IWY Convention in Houston was scheduled for November. We wanted a chance to speak out on issues we knew would be considered there—issues we strongly opposed such as: federally funded day care centers, an end to the discrimination against lesbians and homosexuals, abortion on demand, and the ratification of the ERA. Because we did not want to see such issues passed, we realized it was time to speak up.

"Our pastor gave approval for a Sunday afternoon rally. About 500 women attended. Joyce Rogers spoke on the biblical role of women, Marilyn Simmons spoke on the IWY, and I spoke on ERA. After the rally, women wrote hundreds of letters to their congressman informing them that the women supporting those issues were not representative of all the women in Tennessee. Tapes of this rally were made available for distribution to others."

Sarah reached to women outside her church. "I asked a friend to have a coffee and invited Marilyn to come to Memphis to speak to a group of pastors' wives and leaders from many different churches in our area.

"The pyramid plan is an informative and effective method of communication. Invite key people to a large coffee or tea with the best speaker you can find. Then ask each of them to have a meeting in her home, inviting at least nine others to hear a speaker there. From those nine women, ask at least two to have coffees of their own with a speaker or tape.

"Another idea is to ask key leaders from each church and Bible class in your city to come hear a main speaker. Then ask those who are willing to plan a meeting of their church group or Bible class for which you will provide a speaker. The idea is to get the word to the women!"

Lobbying

In the summer of 1978, Sarah and a group of women flew to Washington to lobby against the time extension for the ratification of the ERA (A week earlier 100,000 women had marched in favor of the extension.) She recalls, "As we waited in line to enter the House Judiciary Committee hearing, the guard at the door said, 'You ladies are so different from the women who were here last week.' We were not sure exactly what he meant, but we had determined, as a group, to behave as God's women, and to seek to represent the Lord Jesus effectively. We wanted everyone we contacted to know that we were happy to be women, and that we delighted in fulfilling our God-given roles."

The time extension was approved. During that summer thousands of women went to Washington to register their opposition to the time extension, but not all on the same date. The group from Memphis came home convinced of the value of numbers. They realized anew that like-minded women needed to develop ways to work together for maximum effectiveness. Later in September many did come together in Washington for a special effort.

"Around the country Christian women are waking up to what is going on and *they* are coming together to join forces effectively. What about you? Where do you fit into the picture of this battle against moral pollution? Generals and foot soldiers are badly needed!"

Between Jobs

Often during these seven years, the Lord would shut the door to active involvement for Sarah Maddox outside her home and church. But she is quick to tell you, "If you neglect your family while you are fighting to protect it, you are defeating your purpose, and you gain nothing."

It was during one of those "between jobs" times that the Lord spoke to Sarah about a unique task He had in mind for her. One day Sarah and Joyce Rogers, her pastor's wife, were sharing their concerns for our country and its future. Their earnest question was, "Lord, where do we go from here? What do we do next?"

As they conversed, Joyce shared with Sarah a special insight. "I believe we ought to work where our sphere of influence is the greatest," Joyce said. This advice was similar to Nehemiah's instructions to his builders to work on the wall nearest to their homes. Where was their influence the greatest? Among Southern Baptists!

"It was true," Sarah says, "that I had been disturbed at the low level of Southern Baptist involvement in Tennessee in combating feminism. The Churches of Christ in Tennessee had gotten 5,000 women to go to the Pro-Family Rally in Houston at the time of the November IWY Convention. Hundreds of women had ridden in buses all night to Washington to lobby against ERA. The Baptists had not been widely represented, and it was my desire to see many Baptist women informed about current issues and events and to be motivated into action and involvement. As we visited and talked about ways to help our women, the idea of having a Christian Women's Concerns Conference was born."

Sarah and Joyce discussed a location and other details, then parted, committing themselves to pray earnestly for God's guidance. The two ladies conferred with their husbands who gave their 100 percent approval.

Therefore, under the leadership of the Holy Spirit and with the encouragement of their husbands, Sarah and Joyce secured speakers and launched publicity for a conference in May 1980. Imagine having the opportunity to hear Elisabeth Elliott, Millie Dienert, Vonette

Bright, Beverly LaHaye and many others who were willing to speak out about concerns of women—and all in one weekend!

"In all the preparations for the conference, we could see the Lord's hand at work. One special blessing was the way in which God worked it out for us to have a well-known Southern Baptist pastor's wife in the leadership of this conference. At the 1979 SBC Annual Meeting, Dr. Adrian Rogers, our pastor, was elected president of the convention. His wife Joyce was the chairman of the Women's Concerns Conference. God's perfect timing is exciting and He is incredibly thorough in meeting our needs superabundantly!"

FLAIR

And there are new ideas on the horizon. The word *flair* has taken on new significance as Sarah Maddox is praying about organizing a group in Memphis to meet a new and demanding need: FLAIR stands for Family Life and Individual Responsibility toward God. Its purpose would be to disseminate information concerning the moral pollution in our country and to suggest concrete ways that Christians can stand *against* evil and stand *for* God and His purposes.

Sarah's activities in the spring of 1980 included speaking out against drafting women and serving as a delegate to the Tennessee Governor's Conference on the Family in Nashville, Tennessee, a prelude to the White House Conference on the Family.

Sarah Maddox has her priorities set. She has made the decision to put other things aside to "fulfill what I believe is God's call, and what His plan is for me right now at this time in my life. Because my greatest desire is to glorify Him and to do His will; 'Where He leads me, I will follow.'"

Building Blocks You Can Place

Political Influence

1. Pray, pray, and pray! Bring our country and its leadership daily before the Lord.

2. Become involved in your local political process. Attend precinct caucuses. Possibly consider volunteering to run for office.

3. Be sure you are registered to vote, encourage others to register, and then vote in every election!

4. Write to Leadership Foundation and find out how you can form a Community Standards' Committee in your area.

5. Write to your elected legislators to tell them your views on bills under consideration.

6. See Irene Conlan's specific suggestions for action in Chapter 20.

7. Additional resources:

Eagle Forum (Phyllis Schlafly), Box 618, Alton, Illinois 62002.

Leadership Foundation (Martha Rountree), 4808 Cleveland Park Station, Washington, D.C. 20008.

The Christian Action Council, 788 National Press Building, Washington, D.C. 20045.

The NAE Office of Public Affairs (Robert Dugan, Director), 1430 K St., N.W., Washington, D.C. 20005.

Campus Ministry

1. Prayerfully and financially support those who minister to college students.

2. Encourage your church to equip students and prospective students for living and witnessing on a college campus.

3. Additional resources:

Navigators, P.O. Box 20, Colorado Springs, Colorado 80901.

Campus Crusade for Christ, Intl., P.O. Box 1576, San Bernardino, California 92402.

Inter-Varsity Christian Fellowship, 233 Langdon St., Madison, Wisconsin 53703.

International Students, Inc., P.O. Box "C," Colorado Springs, Colorado 80901.

Conclusion

Why Don't You Do Something?

In a recent issue of the *Presbyterian Journal,* James Kennedy, pastor of the Coral Ridge Church of Fort Lauderdale, Florida, compared the condition in America today with Nehemiah's day. Dr. Kennedy spoke of the need, then and now, to rebuild the walls.

My friends, I have, as it were, recently examined the walls of America which, unlike the walls of Jerusalem, are virtually invisible to the citizens of this nation.

I have this to report to you: Our walls are fallen down and our gates are burned with fire! . . . I believe that today America stands on the very threshold of total destruction or abject surrender. We are in graver peril than we ever have been before. . . .

It is ironic that unlike Jerusalem our walls were not torn down by the hostile forces of some modern Nebuchadnezzar, but were cast down block by block by the leaders of our own country!

We have thrown away our spiritual foundation and heritage and now we have blind leaders who do not understand what is happening. They have totally misread the designs of our enemies because they are blinded to spiritual truth. Because they do not understand the biblical teaching concerning the nature of man.

The time is very short. We need to pray, as we see the walls in shambles. We need to weep and fast. We need to pray God to forgive this people for its sins. We need to call upon the leaders of this country to rise up and build the walls of this nation ("The Spiritual State of the Union," *Presbyterian Journal,* January 16, 1980).

Can You Trust God?

If you have seen the crumbling walls surrounding our nation and our homes, can you believe that God is sending you to build? Can you trust Him for direction to the right place for you to rebuild the walls?

Can you trust Him for physical and spiritual protection? Can you expect God to make good on His promise to provide all that you need for life and godliness, even while you are experiencing the exertions and challenges of rebuilding?

To each is given a bag of tools, a timepiece, and a book of rules.

Each must make, 'ere his day is done, a stumbling block or a stepping-stone.

Many years ago, these words were the basis for a message delivered by General Kitching of the Salvation Army. The couplet has surfaced in my mind, every once in a while, especially as I ponder life's choices and their potential impact on my life and on the lives of those I influence. Do I really have all the necessary building tools to construct stepping-stones? To rebuild the walls in my God-ordained location?

Information is one essential tool. In this time of urgency, we need to inform ourselves with intelligent precision. We need to be careful about our sources, and prayerful that we will accurately interpret what we read and hear. We need dedication to obey the call of God and to do what is needed near our own homes.

"What can we do?" asks Dr. Kennedy. "Jerusalem was rebuilt in two ways: The walls were rebuilt and the Word of God was proclaimed to bring about revival in the hearts of the people and renewed commitment to the Law of God. This is what we need today" ("The Spiritual State").

As the women of America, you and I have our part in this large and necessary responsibility. It belongs to us, for we are the people of the 80s.

Suggested Reading List

Anderson, Margaret. *Louise.* Wheaton, Ill.: Harold Shaw, 1977.

Angus, Fay. *The Catalyst.* Wheaton, Ill.: Tyndale House, 1979.

Angus, Fay. *Up to Heaven, Down to Earth.* Glendale, Calif.: Regal Books, 1977.

Angus, Fay. *The White Pagoda.* Wheaton, Ill.: Tyndale House, 1978.

Bright, Vonette Z. *For Such a Time as This.* Old Tappan, N.J.: Fleming H. Revell, 1976.

Brown, Harold O.J. *Death Before Birth.* Nashville: Thomas Nelson, Inc., 1977.

Bryant, Anita. *The Anita Bryant Story.* Old Tappan, N.J.: Fleming H. Revell, 1979.

Bryant, Anita, and Green, Bob. *At Any Cost.* Old Tappan, N.J.: Fleming H. Revell, 1978.

Conlan, Irene. *Women, We Can Do It!* Glendale, Calif.: Regal Books, 1976.

Elliot, Elisabeth. *Let Me Be a Woman.* Wheaton, Ill.: Tyndale House, 1976.

Fraiberg, Selma. *Every Child's Birthright: In Defense of Mothering.* New York: Bantam Books, Inc., 1979.

Gallagher, Neil. *How to Stop the Porno Plague.* Minneapolis: Bethany Fellowship, 1977.

Gross, Beatrice, and Gross, Ronald, eds. *The Children's Rights Movement: Overcoming the Oppression of Young People.* Garden City, N.Y.: Doubleday and Co., Inc., 1977.

Hefley, James C. *Textbooks on Trial.* Wheaton, Ill.: Victor Books, 1976.

————, *Humanist Manifestos I and II.* (Introduction by Paul Kurtz) Buffalo, N.Y.: Prometheus Books, 1973.

Johnson, Barbara. *Where Does a Mother Go to Resign?* Minneapolis: Bethany Fellowship, 1979.

Koop, C. Everett. *The Right to Live: The Right to Die.* Wheaton, Ill.: Tyndale House, 1976.

LaHaye, Beverly. *How to Develop Your Child's Temperament.* San Diego: Creation-Life, n.d.

LaHaye, Beverly. *The Spirit-Controlled Woman.* Irvine, Calif.: Harvest House, 1976.

LaHaye, Tim. *The Unhappy Gays.* Wheaton, Ill.: Tyndale House, 1978.

Meeks, Cathy. *I Want Somebody to Know My Name.* Nashville: Thomas Nelson, Inc., 1978.

Nathanson, Bernard. *Aborting America.* Garden City, N.Y.: Doubleday and Co., Inc., 1979.

Pape, Dorothy R. *In Search of God's Ideal Woman: A Personal Examination of the New Testament.* Downers Grove, Ill.: InterVarsity Press, 1976.

Philpott, Kent. *The Third Sex?* Plainfield, N.J.: Logos International, 1975.

Schaeffer, Francis A. *How Should We Then Live?* Old Tappan, N.J.: Fleming H. Revell, 1976.
Schaeffer, Francis A., and Koop, C. Everett. *Whatever Happened to the Human Race?* Old Tappan N.J.: Fleming H. Revell, 1979.
Schlafly, Phyllis. *A Choice Not an Echo.* Alton, Ill.: Pere Marquette Press, 1964.
Schlafly, Phyllis. *The Power of the Positive Woman.* New Rochelle, N.Y.: Arlington House, 1977.
Schlafly, Phyllis. *Power of the Positive Women.* New York: BJ Publishing Group, 1978.
White, John. *Parents in Pain.* Downers Grove, Ill.: InterVarsity Press, 1979.
Wright, Linda R. *Raising Children.* Wheaton, Ill.: Tyndale House, 1975.

Newsletters, Booklets, and Periodicals

The Christian Inquirer, P.O. Box 76, Ellicott Station, Buffalo, New York 14205.
Christians Be Watchful, by Vickie Frierson and Ruthanne Garlock, 1978, Texas Eagle Forum, Box 8253, Dallas, Texas 75205.
Family Protection Report, 4 Library Court, S.E., Washington, D.C. 20003.
Family America, Inc., 418 C St., N.E., Washington, D.C. 20002.
Healing for the Homosexual, published by the Presbyterian Charismatic Communion.
Human Events periodical, 422 First Street, S.E., Washington, D.C. 20003.
Morality in Media, 475 Riverside Drive, New York, N.Y. 10027.
National Affairs Seminar, 1700 Pennsylvania Ave., N.W., Suite 630, Washington, D.C. 20006, Attn: J.T. Houk. Write for information on future seminars.
The National Decency Reporter, Citizens for Decency through Law, 450 Leader Building, Cleveland, Ohio 44114.
National Federation for Decency, Box 1398, Tupelo, Mississippi 38801.
The Right Woman, Congressional News for Women and the Family, 919 18th St., N.W., Washington, D.C. 20006.
Washington Report, published by the Chamber of Commerce of the United States. Available by subscription, $25 for two years.